ABOUT THE AUTHOR

Wilfred Bockelman has spent his adult life in the area of Christian Communications, first as a pastor and then as a writer and editor for Christian magazines. He is a graduate of Capitol University, Evangelical Lutheran Theological Seminary, and Columbia University Graduate School of Journalism. His advanced degrees in Theology and Journalism have been invaluable in his present writing ministry. He is steadily contributing articles to a variety of Christian periodicals and is the author of several pamphlets, among them are *A Church Copes With Change, A New Look at Worship*, and *This We Say; This We Do*. His two books on leadership training have been widely read: *It Will Be Your Duty . . .* , and *You Can Make It Happen*. Wilfred Bockelman is also the founder and editor of *The Eye of the Needle*, a monthly newsletter that seeks to give the proper perspective to religion and morality in the news.

Since 1974 he has served as Director of Communication Research and Special Projects for The American Lutheran Church.

GOTHARD

The Man And His Ministry:

An Evaluation

GOTHARD

The Man And His Ministry:

An Evaluation

by Wilfred Bockelman

PUBLISHED BY
QUILL PUBLICATIONS.

DISTRIBUTED BY
MOTT MEDIA.
POST OFFICE BOX 236
MILFORD MICHIGAN 48042.

Published by
Quill Publications, Editorial Offices: 1260 Coast Village
    Circle, Santa Barbara, CA 93108
Distributed by
Mott Media, Post Office Box 236, Milford, Michigan 48042

Library of Congress Cataloging in Publication Data

Bockelman, Wilfred.
    Gothard: the man and his ministry.

    1. Gothard, Bill. 2. Clergy—United States—Biog-
raghy. 3. Church work with youth. 4. Youth—Religious
life.
BR1725.G7B6   267'.61'0924 [B]   76-43001
ISBN 0-916608-07-7

Cover Design by Rod Burke

TABLE OF CONTENTS

PUBLISHER'S PREFACE

A preface should explain why a book has been written. And that is easy enough to explain.

Bill Gothard is one of the most influential figures in the seventies. He is a towering and controversial figure in the American religious community. His super seminars, the Institute in Basic Youth Conflicts, have been attended by thousands of enthusiastic participants. What those participants hear has been the object of intense and ongoing controversy as well as acclaim. Gothard yes? Gothard no? Chain of command? Interpretation of scripture? What is *really* taught? Who should attend?

It was time for someone to take a look at the man and his ministry and attempt to clarify what is taught, who is helped, and why there is either great loyalty or great scorn for Gothard and his teachings—and seldom anything in between.

For those who want to understand the amazing ministry of this man, who want the real measure of his teachings, and who want to share his innovative Bible teachings with their families and friends, a book was needed.

And so a publisher makes a decision to do a book, the first evaluative study of Bill Gothard's ministry, his influence, and his place in the religious society.

And a skilled researcher and writer is selected.

And then Bill Gothard himself is informed.

While gently embarrassed (appalled?) at the thought of a book about his ministry, he is not hesitant about indicating his reservations about cooperating in any way with its writing. He doesn't want the book. His reasons are discussed later in these pages. But as the weeks pass and the research and writing go on, it is obvious to Gothard that there will be a book. At this point it may be unnecessary to state what is becoming obvious: the resulting book is neither "commissioned" nor "authorized" by Gothard. It is a totally independent project.

A tough job, but a clearly laid out one. And we have succeeded.

The publisher and Gothard have spent hours on the telephone discussing the impact of this book on the reader. The publisher feels that the book will be helpful to both those who have attended Gothard seminars in clarifying the teachings and to those who are considering attending. But Gothard disagrees. Because the book is critical of some things that he teaches, he feels that the book may have a bad effect on the reader.

This conclusion led him to feel he ought not to assist in the rewriting of the rough draft of the book when it was submitted to him.

There was a very positive result in all of this, though. Gothard stated that he felt the Lord was using this experience to pressure him into publishing his own book on the ministry of the Institute in Basic Youth Conflicts. And that's marvelous! We all will look forward to reading it.

In the meantime this book attempts to penetrate the public image and identify the apparent contradictions of this unusual man and his ministry, identify his key ideas, and identify the extent of his influence. It is, I hope, a critical examination and presentation of a man who is important and well worth listening to in person.

One last important point. In all of this I found Gothard to be incredibly sensitive to human beings and their needs, and a man who takes criticism calmly. As busy as he always was, on several occasions he took time to discuss differences with me. He has given much thought to his ministry, to man and his relationship to God, and to the basic problems of alienation, authority, and family relationships.

And now, Bill Gothard. The man and his ministry. An evaluation.

Ben Johnson
Publisher

Chapter 1

WHY A BOOK ABOUT BILL GOTHARD?

The Institute in Basic Youth Conflicts

It was in April of 1973 in the parking lot across the street from my office that I first heard of Bill Gothard. A colleague parked his car beside mine and as we walked to the office together, he said, "You ought to be in St. Paul these nights. There are 8,000 people there every night listening to a three-hour lecture by Bill Gothard."

My retort was, "Bill who?" I thought I read the papers rather carefully, and I had seen neither articles nor ads about him. I was to learn later that this absence of promotion was by design. All 8,000 people going to St. Paul every night that week had heard about Bill Gothard by word of mouth in the same way I had heard about it just then on the way from the parking lot to the office.

"If you can't go this time, maybe you can go next fall when he'll be back in town," my colleague said as we parted to go to our individual offices.

He did remind me in the fall, to tell me that this time there were 16,000 attending the lectures. I still didn't go, but I got a few more facts. Even though the gathering was called Institute in Basic Youth Conflicts, there were more adults in attendance than youth. It was also spoken of as a seminar, but I had a little difficulty envisioning 16,000 people as a seminar. I don't recall if I had a schedule conflict or what, but as I say, I still didn't go.

When Gothard came back to the Twin Cities in April of 1974, it was predicted that he would draw an attendance of 27,500. By now articles were beginning to appear about him in the paper. Also, in the meantime I had gotten a new assignment in my work. I was made director of communication research of The American Lutheran Church.

I told my supervisor that anybody who can attract 27,500 people for a 32-hour lecture program during a six-day week knows something about communication we ought to research—all the more so when these 27,500 pay $45 ($35 if they register in groups in advance) to hear these lectures by Gothard and when many of his most dedicated followers admit that he is at best a second-rate speaker.

One of the most remarkable features of the seminars is that there are no great promotional campaigns to announce them. Gothard trusts that the Lord will bring those who should come. And the fact that so many did come without the influence of four-color posters, television spots on prime time, and newspaper ads suggested that Gothard was worthy of a closer look.

Added to that was the fact that many of the members of our own congregations were chartering buses and taking groups of 50 and 100, some driving as far as 100 miles and driving back home again after the lecture closed at 10. Gothard had become a phenomenon and it was part of my job to go and hear him. Besides, I was personally curious about what made him tick and why he had such a following. I hadn't heard enough particulars about him to be prejudiced either negatively or positively, so I went with as much of a clean-slate frame of mind as it is possible to have.

I recalled the national youth conventions I had attended in my earlier years. They had had a profound impression on me. The singing of rousing hymns, the thrill of being part of a large group committed to the Lord was an inspiring experience in my life.

Some of that thrill came back to me as I walked into the Civic Center Auditorium in St. Paul on that April Monday night in 1974 to attend my first evening of the Institute in Basic Youth Conflicts. I'm enough of an old "conservative" never to have let my heart catch up with my mind in accepting the "hippie" mode of dress. So it was doubly satisfying to savor the nostalgia of the good old days when straight people went to huge religious gatherings.

I arrived at the auditorium half an hour early, but already the seats were at a premium. People had brought sack lunches and soft drinks and were eating and drinking at their seats. I had to sit all the way across the auditorium from the speaker's podium, so that Gothard himself seemed hardly more than postage stamp size. The sound system was excellent, and he had an overhead projector that threw huge images on a screen, so the message was absolutely clear.

By the second night, I learned, however, that it was better to watch the lecture in an adjacent auditorium where it was brought by closed circuit television to an overflow crowd of 5,000. There it was possible to get a much better vision of Gothard himself as he was speaking and catch the fuller nuances of his facial features.

Admission was by name card only, which you received when you paid your registration. You also received a two and one-quarter inch sturdy notebook, and in the middle of each session you received a "chapter" of notes. A card with your name inside the notebook carried this message: "With each set of materials, this card must be presented to the Materials Distribution Center in order for you to secure that day's presentation. Materials *WILL NOT* be given out without this card. Please put it in a safe place and bring it to each session. Duplicates will not be given out." No tape recorders are allowed in the auditorium.

I couldn't help comparing this to a large gathering (some 20,000 people) of our own denomination at the Houston Astrodome the previous summer, when the audience walked out by the hundreds if not thousands if the program of the evening didn't please them. And there the program was high level entertainment in a medium supposedly appealing to youth. Here at the St. Paul Civic Center 27,500 people sat through what might be called a rather prosaic Bible lesson an hour and a half at a stretch, and the only ones who walked out were those who had to go to the bathroom.

From the moment Bill Gothard first came on the stage promptly at 7 o'clock until he quit at 10 o'clock—with the exception of the 20-minute intermission when everyone got materials—there was complete concentration on everything he said. Although his soft voice approaches monotone, it is pleasant to listen to. He's not at all flamboyant. As he speaks he illustrates his lectures with little stick figures that he draws on a sheet and projects on an overhead screen, or he simply writes down key words. But the crowd sits silently and takes it all in with an occasional murmur as they are overwhelmed with the power and simplicity of the scriptural truth that Gothard has to bring.

Two years later I attended the last three days of an Institute in Basic Youth Conflicts seminar in Cobo Hall in Detroit. A year and a half prior to that our own church body had held its national convention there. I recalled the contrast. For instance, our convention opened its daily program with a devotional service, but if you went into the dining hall twenty minutes after the service started you would still find perhaps several hundred people eating breakfast, rather oblivious to the fact that the day's activities were beginning with prayer in the convention hall.

While attending the Institute in Basic Youth Conflicts, which began at 9:30 a.m., I arrived at the dining room one morning at 9:28. There were two people in the dining hall, and they seemed to be on the working staff of the building. More than 8,500 were already in their seats for the 9:30 beginning of the day's activities.

The afternoon schedule of the last day of the seminar is somewhat grueling to say the least. From 1:30 until 7:00 in the evening, there was one break of 20 minutes and one of 30 minutes. Otherwise, that five and one-half hours was filled with solid lecture by one man, Bill Gothard, and there were 8,600 people in rapt attention.

The Institute in Basic Youth Conflicts seminars obviously have something to say about teaching methodologies. Pedagogical theory may be right that you don't really teach or change people very effectively through the lecture method, and that everything has to be in short snippets or people just won't listen. The fact still remains that hundreds of thousands of people sit quietly for three solid hours a night with a 20-minute intermission. So, it isn't a matter of people not listening to lectures. There are lectures and there are lectures. People won't listen to *some* lectures. But they very eagerly listen to other kinds of lectures.

Gothard's Appeal

What is it, then, that causes so many Christians to gain so much from these seminars? One man in whose judgment I have confidence has been to several of Gothard's Institutes and, although he is critical of some of the theological presuppositions, had some very astute observations about why Gothard is so helpful to people.

"Gothard is a master mechanic and a master teacher," he said. "As he lectures he draws very simple illustrations that show how things fit together. This fits with that, and he has a Bible passage to prove it. That fits with something else, and another Bible passage proves that. And this is how these two things fit together into something else, and here's the Scripture that proves that. *The whole thing just fits beautifully.*"

"You can sense the feeling of excitement as Gothard shows how all these things are related. People have always been convinced that the Bible is a good book, and have perhaps had a sense of guilt that they didn't understand it better. Now, here is a man who can put it together for them and put a handle on it so they can grasp it."

This same man said that he had been in the Lutheran Church all his life, and of course he believes in grace and justification and in the fact that this is God's world and we are in God's hands, but he was never able to say just what this meant. After studying with Gothard he feels he now understands and can articulate what he has always held in vague terms to be God's truth. "Now," he asks, "Why wasn't 50 years in the Lutheran Church able to do that for me?"

In this sense Gothard has his finger on the pulse of questions people are asking. He speaks to their problems with authority in a way that the churches have apparently failed to do.

The very fact that the growth of the Institute ministry has been so outstanding and that it has all been by word of mouth rather than by heavily-budgeted promotional programs testifies to the fact that he is meeting some needs. The following are a few instances:

- A husband and wife on the verge of breaking up who insist that the Institute in Basic Youth Conflicts saved their marriage.

- One psychiatrist says he sent 80 of his most difficult cases to Gothard. People who were not being helped by psychiatrists were getting their lives straightened out through the seminars.

- A 27-year-old daughter extremely rebellious against her parents, has a "conversion" experience, is reconciled with them and has gotten them to attend the next seminar when it comes to town.

- A doctor who says that increasingly the patients who come to his office are not physically ill but have a marriage problem. He finds Gothard's lectures as the answer to help them.

- Already deeply committed Christian couples who continue to attend the seminars a second or third time because they find it enriches their life.

- Other Christians who say the seminar provides them with insight on how to overcome bitterness and improve their devotional life.

- Presidents of some corporations who are so convinced of the value of the Institute that they personally pay the registration for any of their employees who want to go.

Some Counter-Examples

A researcher with integrity will, however, be just as insistent on exploring counter-examples. I cannot be deaf to some of the accusations I hear. People involved in the counseling professions tell me that whenever Gothard comes to town they can be certain that their caseload will pick up. That in itself is not a condemnation of Gothard. To use an analogy, I suppose that if there were a group of thieves, and a charismatic speaker came to town and spoke so persuasively against stealing that their consciences became smitten and they sought help from counselors, that wouldn't be altogether bad.

I remember one evening I was talking with a group of people from one church who had all gone to the seminar and discussed with them the pros and cons of the Institute. One of them came to my wife afterwards and said, "I didn't go to the Institute myself, but I just wanted to hear what it was all about. You know, I work for the county mental health clinic, and I know from past experience that we are the ones who get stuck with the people whose thinking and lives have been wrecked by this kind of approach."

Many church leaders I know have questions about the kind of theology espoused by Gothard, even though it was precisely that kind of theology that got them active in the church.

In light of these widely divergent opinions concerning Gothard, I felt that a report concerning him would be helpful to my denomination. When I attended the Gothard Institute in Basic Youth Conflicts in 1974, I wrote a 13-page evaluation entitled "The Pros and Cons of Bill Gothard." Our office duplicated 100 copies of it and sent it to some of the leaders in our church, and I thought I had fulfilled my duties. But we began to get requests from our pastors all over the country for a copy of my evaluation, so that now—without any promotion—we have sent out about 5,000 copies of that mimeographed report.

Someone suggested that I send a copy to *The Christian Century.* The editors asked me to adapt my report for a *Century* article, which I did, and it appeared in the September 25, 1974 issue. I am told that that article had the second highest request for reprints of any article that appeared in the *Century* that year.

Gothard's Opposition to Publicity

Now with all the interest Gothard has aroused in the Christian community, the question can be asked, why wasn't this book written long ago?

It's become legend however that Gothard tries very hard to avoid reporters. He will grant them an interview—I personally had a four-hour interview with him—but he certainly doesn't seek coverage. In fact, he aggressively discourages it.

I know of some evangelical publishers who have turned down offers of authors who have wanted to do a book on Gothard. One of them quite frankly said, "We know that Gothard doesn't want a book published about him, so we're not going to publish one." An evangelical magazine wanted to do an article on Gothard, but cancelled it after a strong suggestion from Gothard that it not be published.

The alumni magazine of Wheaton College, of which Gothard is an illustrious graduate, wanted to do an article—as all college alumni magazines want to do on their outstanding graduates—but they bowed to Gothard's wishes.

In reporting these things I am in no way suggesting that Gothard has something to hide. I am completely persuaded that his motivation is entirely honorable. He has a genuine sense of modesty and humility that is worth emulating.

In light of Gothard's objections, do I as an author have a right to produce a book about him when he himself doesn't particularly care to have the book written? Where is a person's right to privacy? Obviously, Gothard is not a salaried public official whose constituency demands to know all about him. Those who attend his seminars pay the fees and evidently aren't asking for a book about him, for they hear him personally. Do those who aren't involved really have a right to insist on knowing?

Bill Gothard is perfectly justified in saying, "If people want to know what the Institute in Basic Youth Conflicts is all about, let them come to the seminar." He even has a right to say, "You can't form an opinion unless you've attended the whole Institute." He has reason to be dissatisfied with those who have never attended one of his Institutes but who nevertheless pontificate on them.

Still, I don't think Gothard is being particularly reasonable when he suggests that people attending the seminar not even discuss the handbook outside the meettings. In fact, that policy tends to work at counterpurposes with one of his tenets, which is to instill the highest respect for morality. People get together and say to each other, "We're not supposed to be discussing this with anybody, but let's do it anyway." In much the same way there is the understanding that admission is only by your name card obtained at the time of registration, and that this name card is not transferable. I can't imagine that I'm the only one who has heard at least a dozen people say, "I'm not going this evening; why don't you use my card?" All of this at a meeting aimed at inculcating the highest moral code.

Still people are simply people, and they are curious. I suppose Gothard has a right to say, "I'm not going to tell you about myself ahead of time. Pay $35 or $45 and come and hear me for 32 hours and then you'll know what I have to say." However, it's more than idle curiosity for a person to say, "I'd like to know a little more about something before I pay $35 for it."

Also, a study of the Institute in Basic Youth Conflicts and the appeal of Bill Gothard becomes a study of our times. What is there about our times that predisposes people to flock to Gothard's seminars? Would he be equally successful at another time in history, or is there something characteristic about our times that we need to understand?

Gothard is aware, of course, that he cannot keep a book about him from being published, and we both agreed that sooner or later one would be published. His greatest fear about having a book published that does not have his full approval is that his program of Institute in Basic Youth Conflicts will be presented in such a way that other people will want to copy it without knowing its full background. His concern is not whether they will make money on it. His concern is that honest, well-meaning people will try to copy it without understanding all of the basics that go into it.

In order to do our best to avoid misconstruing Gothard's program, the publisher had an hour's telephone conversation with Gary Smalley, generally regarded as the "Number 2 man" in the Gothard organization, and several lengthy telephone conversations with Gothard himself. I, the author, had a 20-minute telephone conversation with Gothard and a four-hour personal interview with him in a home in Detroit in the presence of the chairman of the Detroit Seminar Committee.

In his conversation with Gothard, the publisher promised him the opportunity to see the entire manuscript before publication, to discuss any differences of opinion, to have a chapter or chapters at the beginning or end or in the middle or a whole book to state his case.

Gothard's response to this has been definite. Although this is the first book that has been written about him, several magazine articles have been written about him and in each case the author promised him the same opportunity. But, Gothard says that either the author did not stick to his promise, or else if he did respond, he was told that the article was so far along into publication that nothing could really be done about his comments. Gothard, therefore, is understandably leery about such an author-publisher promise.

Doing Things God's Way

The most important reason, however, why Gothard opposes this book is based on his conviction that a printed critical evaluation (pro and con) of any Christian is inappropriate.

"It's not a matter of being fair or objective," Gothard says. "It's a matter of doing it God's way."

And he finds God's way described in Matthew 18: 15-18 and Galatians 6:1. The gist of Matthew 18 is that if someone has wronged you, your first obligation is to go to him personally and discuss the situation. If the difference cannot be reconciled, then take along two or three witnesses. If there is still no reconciliation of differences, then take it before the whole church.

Galatians 6:1 says: "Brethren, if a man is overtaken in a fault, ye which are spiritual, restore such a one in the spirit of meekness, considering thyself, lest thou also be tempted."

Gothard feels strongly that the way of the church is not the way of the world, and the way of Christian journalism is not the way of secular journalism. The question is not whether you've been fair, but whether you've done things God's way, and no matter how much an attempt by objective journalism to present the pros and cons may be in vogue, it is still not God's way.

The way for Christians is to present a good report of each other, and if there are differences of opinion, they should be cleared up between the two people involved, or in the presence of several witnesses, and not in public or in public print. He feels uncomfortable, therefore, in being placed in a situation that violates his own convictions concerning the Christian way of arriving at understanding.

"I read your article in the *Christian Century*," he said, "and although I know you tried to be fair, you nevertheless made some accusations against my theology that you should have checked with me personally before you put them in public print. I detected a spirit of antagonism rather than a desire to build up the body of Christ."

I reminded him that I did not insist that I was right and he was wrong, but that my purpose was to discuss openly the pros and cons of a situation so that out of discussion a better understanding might emerge. He insisted, "But that is not God's way."

While he insists that he is not as hard to interview as people seem to think he is, he is skeptical about the purpose for which he is being interviewed. "I'll be glad to talk with anyone who has an honest criticism," he added. "The quickest way to get a reply from me is to write and say, 'I have a criticism.' That is God's way according to Matthew 18. If you want to tell me where I've been wrong, then I want to talk with you. I want to learn. But if you want to talk with me so that you can use what I say in writing a book, that is simply not God's way."

Even though Bill was very friendly and cordial during our entire interview—and I honestly feel we both enjoyed the talk and were both benefited by it, he still confessed to uneasiness about having had the interview. "Because," he said, "now you can say you had an interview with me and that will make it seem that I approved of this method of arriving at truth—openly and publicly discussing differences of opinion, that according to God's way should not be done publicly."

"When two Christians disagree in public," he said, "they provide a bad example for the world. The public already has an image of us as fighting among ourselves. Of the early Christians it was said, 'Behold how they love one another.' We need to give a good report of each other before the world. That's God's way of arriving at understanding."

"There's one way I'd be happy about this book," Gothard said, "and that is if the book itself could become an example of the kind of Christian journalism that would be pleasing to God, if we could agree that the purpose of the book is to build up the body of Christ and not to find fault with the way one person presents it without first talking with him about it. The Christian church and Christian writers are all too prone to follow the way of secular journalists. So they think that if they say some good things about a person and some negative things, they have been objective. The point is that God's way is to give a good report of others, and to deal privately with a person in those areas in which you don't agree."

I personally take that as a challenge, although with a degree of difference at various points. I will grant that sometimes Christian journalists seem to enjoy attacking the theology of someone with whom they do not agree. Christian charity is not always practiced among Christian writers. Christian writers, also being sinful, too often give in to the temptation to choose words for their cutting and tearing ability rather than for their ability to edify. I would hope that this could indeed become a book that might serve as an example of one Christian brother examining the program and theology of another in such a way as to build up the Body of Christ.

Having said that, however, I still have some problems. I, too, read the Bible and try to do things God's way; but since Gothard and I are both human and both fallible we may not always agree as to which is God's way. Nor can I assume that if we just talk together long enough in person we will both agree and can then present a common front.

I'm grateful for the doctrine of grace, which means that we are not dependent for our salvation on the certainty of having right answers. God saves me through Christ, his death and resurrection, and accepts me as I am, not because I have the right answers. Hopefully, I'll have a large number of right answers, but I am not thereby saved. I am free therefore to explore and even to call into question the answers someone else might give without thereby insisting that I am right and he is wrong.

Nor do I believe that the Bible teaches that when two Christians honestly disagree on something that that will be a sign to the world of the weakness of the church. The world may indeed see that as a strength. There are limits, of course. If two Christians disagreed on everything, the world would have a right to ask questions. Nor can differences be held in a cavalier manner. But two Christians honestly struggling to understand God's word and coming—at least for the time being—to different conclusions does not destroy the witness of the church, not even if the differences are discussed in public. Honesty is also a virtue, and if the world sees two

Christians honestly and lovingly arriving at different points of view on some issues, that can also be a powerful witness.

The Bible itself follows that pattern. The disciples had squabbles among themselves. Paul and John Mark had a parting of the ways. Paul and Peter had a major argument. This is not to say that their actions were in line with God's plans. But the Holy Spirit did not see fit to expunge these accounts from the pages of the scripture. That's what the remarkable grace of God is all about. God uses people who are finite, who in their finiteness will disagree with each other. There are other alternatives besides on the one hand maintaining absolute silence about these differences, or, on the other hand, blowing them out of all proportion or even wallowing in them. There is a responsbile dealing with differences of opinion in such a way that a consideration of these differences will produce growth in understanding. The author pledges himself to that kind of reporting and evaluation.

The situation is not unlike that taking place in the classrooms of more than a thousand Bible schools and seminaries throughout the country. Professors will use textbooks as a tool of instruction, but it is not likely that they will agree with everything written in every textbook. In some instances they may agree with 90% or more of what the author says; in other cases they may agree with only 10%. They will undoubtedly call to the students' attention those portions of the book with which they disagree. This generally does not reflect on the author's personal integrity. It's simply a matter of disagreement—sometimes, to be sure, on very important matters, but sometimes on secondary matters.

It would be virtually impossible for every one of these professors in the more than 1,000 schools to feel that they could not discuss these differences of opinion with students unless they first went to the authors personally and discussed the matter with them according to Matthew 18 or Galatians 6:1. We feel that these two passages were written for situations within a congregation where people had actually wronged each other—"sinned against," as Matthew said. When I say that I don't agree with Bill Gothard on a particular matter, I am not saying that he has sinned against me. I'm not even saying he's wrong. I will very likely say that *I think* he is wrong, and then state as best as possible my understanding of what he is trying to say and why I disagree.

Gothard would like to see more people play the part of Priscilla and Aquila in the book of Acts, who quietly went about behind the scenes and corrected Apollos when he made exaggerated statements. He thinks there is altogether too much tendency to want to rush into public print whenever there is a disagreement. This may be good secular journalism, but it's not good Christian journalism, Gothard says. Granted, patient, behind-the-scenes teaching is always in order, but in the mass society we have today the Priscilla and Aquila approach can also exhibit itself in a responsible book that honestly examines differences of opinion.

In light of these considerations I feel that a book about Gothard is justified even though he objects. When someone becomes a public figure—inside or outside of the church—whether he likes it or not, he will be the subject of public interest. This book is not intended to appease the curiosity seeker. I pledge myself to honest and responsible reporting as well as to a genuine commitment to the upbuilding of the Body of Christ, in order to provide Christians with information that will help them become mature in their discernment of where believers disagree, and self-critical of their own effectiveness for God.

Even if we would finally decide that Gothard's approach leaves much to be desired, that in itself would not free us from the necessity of asking what we are doing that is better. We are reminded of a comment attributed to Dwight L. Moody. It went something like this: "I like my way of doing it better than your way of not doing it." If we don't like Gothard's way of doing it, are we doing it any better or are we just doing nothing?

A decision, then, to publish a book about Gothard is not to do an analysis just for the sake of analysis. Its intention is to be helpful—hopefully, helpful to Gothard himself—but also to the critics of Gothard who find his approach lacking but thus far have seemingly not come up with anything better.

And I have every confidence in Gothard that his first interest is in helping people and not insisting that *he* be the one to help them. If this book, therefore, can aid churches in their regular program to do what Gothard would like to see done, I imagine that Gothard would be the first to praise God.

While this book will be critical of some of Gothard's approaches, it will be equally critical of those who would easily write him off. Precisely because his program is so comprehensive, it is easier to understand it in manageable parts. Human nature being what it is, those parts that draw the most attention are often those that seem most bizarre or most at variance with commonly held beliefs. In a day of emphasis on women's liberation, therefore, Gothard's strong insistence on the chain of command, which puts the wife under the authority of the husband, attracts a lot of attention. It would be unfortunate, however, if the whole approach were written off simply because of objection to parts of it.

The purpose of this book is to put Gothard in perspective.

Chapter 2

WHAT ABOUT
GOTHARD HIMSELF?

Relatively Little Is Known About Bill Gothard

The most striking feature about Gothard as a public figure is his desire to remain anonymous.

"I feel best when I am unrecognized," he said. "When I go into a restaurant in a city where a seminar is being held and I am not recognized, I feel good about that. I feel even better when I overhear others at a nearby table say, 'What's that guy's name who's speaking down at the auditorium and drawing such huge crowds?' "

Very little is known about his early life; in fact, a director of a syndicated news service said about him, "even his birth is mysterious." This is in no sense to be taken as though there is something unseemly about his background. It simply underscores the fact that Gothard doesn't think it's necessary to talk about it.

The incidents that he does tell from time to time are quite in line with his whole philosophy of life, which is that events are important only as they impinge on a person's relationship with God; or, to put it in another way, events are worth noting only if God used them to shape one's character.

The following snippets of information about his early life are gleaned from anecdotes that he tells about himself and his family in the seminar lectures. There's no doubt about it, he grew up in a deeply religious family, and his father set an example for him that has influenced him throughout the years.

His father was slated to become the president of a company, and on the day he was to have been named to the position, he decided not to take it because he learned that he would have to compromise a principle. So without having another job to go to, he gave up the chance to be a corporation president.

Later, as a relatively new convert to Christianity, he moved into a position with Gideon's International in the late 40's. The Gideons had undergone a crisis in their ranks at that time and lost the two top men in their organization. Gothard's father, who had a background in publications, was brought in to serve as editor of the organization's publication and also as executive of Gideon's.

According to an interview with a former associate of William Gothard, senior, as reported in *The Wittenburg Door,* the Gideons were greatly understaffed at the time and the elder Gothard was a hard worker. He arrived at 8:00 in the morning and often worked till 11:00 or midnight. In the words of his associate, the elder Gothard "was a real work horse, and yet he refused to hire people until he was sure that these were the people God wanted him to hire for the organization. The one bright spot in the daily one and a half hour staff meetings was Gothard's daily tales of witnessing. He would pick up hitchhikers every morning on the way to work, witness to them and give them tracts. He had glowing stories to tell and was very enthusiastic."

Gothard as a Student

Young Bill was not a very good student in his early years in school. In his own delightfully humorous style he tells the story of how his teacher called him into the hall toward the end of the first grade. Bill was surprised to find his mother in the hall too.

The teacher's message was something like this: "Now Bill, wouldn't you like to stay in the first grade another year and be a leader in the class next year?"

"So I volunteered to be a leader," says Bill. "The only problem was that at the end of the next year I was offered the job as volunteer leader again. But they decided they couldn't keep me in the first grade forever, so I was passed on probation. Those words, 'passed on probation' were on my report card for nine years straight."

To put it mildly, Bill was a poor student. And he remained a poor student until he got into high school. Then a friend suggested to him that he memorize scripture; but poor memory had been the cause of his bad grades all along. He promised his friend he'd try, for there was nothing to lose. He spent 17 hours the first week memorizing scripture. He very quickly moved from the step of memorizing scripture to meditating on it and seeing how it applied to his daily life. His grades immediately went to A, and they stayed there as long as he spent 17 hours a week memorizing and meditating. When he felt he didn't have that much time to devote to meditating, his grades went down.

This experience left such an impact on Gothard that he has built his whole life on this principle. He likes to ask his audiences as well as individuals with whom he talks, "If I could tell you how to guarantee that everything you do will prosper, would you be interested?" And then he tells them, "There is a clearcut Bible text for this guarantee. Psalm 1:3: 'The blessed man,' says the Psalmist, 'meditates on the law of God day and night and *whatsoever he doeth shall prosper.*' "

"You may not have success as the world defines success," Gothard adds, but he makes this Biblical promise sound compelling for achieving success in God's eyes.

At an early age Gothard had a conversion experience. He often tells of struggling against unclean thoughts and being unable to put them aside. One day he committed himself completely to Christ and gained the assurance that Christ was his personal saviour. He says that the experience was like going from death to life. From that time on he depended completely on God for guidance in his life.

He attended Wheaton College, and decided that he wanted to go into full-time Christian work, but the only two occupations he could think of in that category were the ministry or a call to the mission field. He didn't feel he was cut out for either one. He didn't want to be a minister because he was afraid of speaking to crowds. (This always brings a chuckle from his thousands of listeners.) And he didn't want to become a missionary because he didn't like to travel. (This brings another chuckle from the crowds, who are mindful of his seminar in all parts of the country.)

Bill was ordained in the LaGrange Bible Church in suburban Chicago and still attends services there when he is not on the road, but his real ministry has become youth work. At last count he had declined three offers of honorary doctor's degrees.

Early Ministry as a Youth Worker

An opportunity opened up for him to become a youth worker for a local missionary society in Chicago. He devoted 35 hours a week to youth work while still a student at Wheaton. However, he tells that his deep devotion to youth work also caused him to be proud and that other members of the staff resented his pride. One day Bill learned of this resentment. Always conscientious about having right attitudes, Bill went to one person to make amends and confess his pride.

"I honestly expected him to say, 'Oh, that's all right, Bill. It's not that bad. Don't worry about it,' " Bill says. But it didn't happen that way. Not only did the fellow worker underscore the fact that Bill was developing an attitude of pride, but he gave him a list of people to whom he ought to confess his pride. One of those was the director of the mission society that employed Bill. Fully ready to make amends, Bill went to the director and confessed his pride.

The director was impressed, so much so that he broke into tears. "I'm glad you came to me," the director said. "I accept your apology and forgive you, but nevertheless I'm going to go through with what I think I have to do." The next day the director called Bill in and told him that he was fired.

Bill was stunned. He thought his work had been acceptable, and he couldn't imagine that his attitude of pride had been that much of a factor or that obvious. To make matters worse, the position went to the new staff member who had first told Bill about his problem with pride.

But Bill looks back on that experience now as one of the important milestones in his life. It forced him to examine himself rigorously. It also caused him to be sensitive to other people who suffer severe blows in life, many of them unexpected and, at first, seemingly unjustified. The experience made Bill all the more dependent upon God, that if He closes one door, He opens another. Through all this, Bill felt himself called into a more extensive and intensive youth ministry.

In the early 50's Bill was active in youth work in the Chicago area, working with gangs as well as church youth groups. He had developed an amazing facility for giving chalk talks and usually found young people willing to come and watch and listen. A call to commitment to the Lord always held a prominent place in his presentations.

He was not above using some manipulative devices in shaping the thinking of youth, and he justifies it on the basis that the young people themselves often thank him afterwards and say it was this precise event that taught them to take the Lord seriously.

He tells the story of how one day he asked a church youth group if they would like to see an honest-to-goodness gang. They were impressed and followed him through the streets to where they would meet a gang. Just before they got to the place where they were to meet the gang, Bill told them, "There's one thing I forgot to tell you. One thing about these gangs is that they can spot a phony and a hypocrite a mile off. So if there are any of you who are not right with the Lord and aren't really dedicated to him even though you are a member of a church group, you better not go around the corner with me. The gang will spot you for being what you are, and if there is one thing they don't like it's hypocrites."

There was some heavy breathing among his youth group as well as a diminution in number. As he tells this story at his seminar, a roll of amused and approving laughter runs through the audience, and there are nods of sanction as Bill tells them that years later he received a letter from one of these boys—now a minister—who credits this experience for having brought him closer to the Lord.

The Birth of the Seminars

But after ten years of youth work in the Chicago area Gothard became convinced that God was leading him in another direction. He was bothered by the questions: Why do so many teenagers lose their faith during college years? How can lasting results be achieved in youth work? During the next five years he spent much time in homes of teenagers and observed their family life.

In an interview with *The Wittenburg Door,* a magazine published in California, Gary Smalley, midwest director of Institute in Basic Youth Conflicts, described Gothard's years in youth work this way:

"When he was in high school and college working with gangs in Chicago and so on, a lot of the kids he worked with washed out. And it was real discouraging to him. Then he began to go into the homes. He went right into the home and began to see cause and effect. He'd see a certain kid doing these few things and see the effect in his life. So Bill began to hook the cause and effect with the Biblical principles and found out that they were consistent. He found out that if a person was really bitter and resentful toward his or her mother and father, certain things would happen in his life. He found that evidenced in scripture too. And then he began to see that a lot of these things hooked up. It was around 1963 or 1964, somewhere around in there, he went up to a camp in summer he was asked to teach a class at Wheaton College. Forty-five pastors, youth workers, educators, and students were in the class. This essentially was the beginning of the seminar.

Bill feels that these were important years in his ministry and that a sizable chapter could be written on them. (The reason nothing has been written for publication on these years is that no one has taken the time to do the research on them. Bill feels the best people to talk to are the many people who were involved with him—parents, churches, the youth themselves.) "Many of the things we learned during these years—both what to do and what not to do—gave us insights that became part of our handbook for the Institute in Basic Youth Conflicts," says Bill.

In 1964 Bill began to share his insights with fifteen youth workers and during this time he summarized the principles and put them into a growing syllabus. The following summer he was asked to teach a class at Wheaton College. Forty-five pastors, youth workers, educators, and students were in the class. This essentially was the beginning of the seminar.

The Rapid Growth of the Seminars

He conducted a seminar in 1966 and 1967, with 1,000 people in attendance at each one. In 1968, at the insistence of a Washington dentist, he held his first out-of-town seminar in Seattle, where 42 attended. Total attendance at seminars during 1968 was 2,000. Then the increases started. In 1969 there were 4,000; 1971, 12,000; 1972 over 128,000, including 13,000 in the Seattle Coliseum; in 1973 more than 200,000, including 16,000 in Los Angeles, 17,000 in Seattle, 8,000 in Chicago, 8,000 in Philadelphia, and 20,000 in Dallas. The introductory chapter of this book told of the growth in St. Paul-Minneapolis alone: from 8,000 in the spring of 1973, to 12,000 in the fall of that year, to 27,500 in the spring of 1974. 35,000 had been predicted for the fall of 1974, but the attendance dropped to 22,000.

If the attendance keeps growing as it has been, Gothard's seminars will have reached an audience equivalent to the population of the United States by 1981. The demand has become so great that arrangements are made for closed circuit television when the audience is too big for the largest auditorium in a city. Seminars also can be aired by network delayed telecast to cities. (For instance, at the same time I was attending a seminar in Detroit where Gothard was appearing in person, a video-taped program of his lectures was being seen and heard in Hershey, Pennsylvania.)

Thirty-two seminars, featuring either a personal appearance of Gothard or a network delayed telecast, were scheduled at the following places during 1976 (asterisk indicates network delayed telecast):

April 12-17	Memphis, Tenn.*
April 19-24	Los Angeles, Calif.
April 19-24	Bakersfield, Calif.*
April 26-May 1	Eugene, Ore.*
May 10-15	Houston, Tex.*
May 10-15	Tampa, Fla.*
May 17-22	Forth Worth, Tex.
May 17-22	Phoenix, Ariz.*
May 24-29	Detroit, Mich.
May 24-29	Hershey, Penn.*
June 7-12	New Haven, Conn.*
June 14-19	Atlanta, Ga.
June 21-26	Washington D.C.
June 21-26	Ocean Grove, N.H.*
July 5-10	Portland, Ore.
July 12-17	Seattle, Wash.
July 12-17	Spokane, Wash.*
July 19-24	Philadelphia, Penn.
July 19-24	Indianapolis, Ind.*
July 26-31	Grand Rapids, Mich.*
August 2-7	Chicago, Ill.
August 2-7	Denver, Colo.*
August 23-28	Dallas, Tex.
September 13-18	Oakland, Calif.
October 11-16	Miami Beach, Fla.*
October 11-16	Hempstead, Long Island*

October 24-30	San Diego, Calif.*
November 1-6	St. Paul, Minn.
November 1-6	Fresno, Calif.*
November 8-13	Oklahoma City, Okla.*
November 8-13	Omaha, Neb.*
November 15-20	Austin, Tex.*

During the growing years of the organization a five-man board of directors was organized, and the work was incorporated under the name Campus Teams, Inc. Bill has the title of president and seminar instructor, and fills the position of "chief executive officer."

The board is also responsible for the funds. Fees for the seminar are $45 per person, or $35 if a person is part of a church group. Husband and wife can register for $55. Persons who have registered once for the seminar become alumni and can attend any seminar without paying additional fees. It has been reported that roughly 20% of the total budget is spent for publicity—mostly through alumni; 25% to 30% for staff expenses to develop materials and take care of all the work related to preparation for the seminars; 30% to 40% for future development—television equipment for closed circuit seminars, land purchase if "God allows" the group to build a school. Presumably the board decides where the remaining 10% goes.

Gothard's Personal Life-Style

Gothard now 41 years old, lives on a very modest $600 a month. He is unmarried and lives with his parents. Every now and then a rumor gets started that he is married. He deals with these rumors in good-natured fashion. When people come up to him at a seminar and say, "I'm so glad to hear you were married," he puts them at ease with, "Tell me, who is she?"

He gives two reasons for not being married. "In the first place, the Lord has not made the right person known to me yet. And, I haven't found a free week-end yet."

In one of his lectures he does tell about a date he had with a very popular girl, the ideal of everything he had dreamed of. He asked her for a date, and to his surprise and delight, she accepted. To his even greater surprise when he brought her home, she invited him to some kind of an event, an invitation that he immediately accepted. He never identifies the event and does not intimate that there was anything wrong with it. "But it would have been wrong for *me* to go," he concluded, and so he called the girl up and said that upon thinking it over he decided he could not go. They have remained friends through the years.

Even in telling about this as well as other incidents to which he refers in the seminar he is very seldom judgmental of people with whose standards he differs. He minces no words in denouncing what he thinks are gross immoralities of our day—permissiveness, loose sexual morality, homosexuality, atheistic tendencies fostered in schools, but he can always do it in a tone of voice that shows his tenderness and love for people.

He is opposed to tendencies and life styles that supposedly are "in" with the younger generation—immodest apparel, rock music, dancing—but his method of disapproving is not one of histrionic railing against them, but of gently and firmly stating his convictions and backing them up from scripture.

One of his associates, Gary Smalley, in answering a question put to him by a reporter, "How would you characterize Gothard?" said:

"Well, I'm a little biased, I'm sure. But I don't know that I would be because I think each person on the staff has a fantastic admiration for him. Of all the men I know, he's the most gracious, loving, selfless, considerate, giving. . . . He communicates that selfless, considerate giving to all of us. And he never communicates to any one of us that he doesn't have time for us. He'd give you his clothes right on him, you know, if you needed them. He has often said that his ministry with the seminars is a reflection of what goes on in the office. And we would all agree with that. His life adds up in the office to what he says out there."

Chapter 3

THE BIG RED BOOK

An Overwhelming Source of Information & Instruction

If you're ever in a city and you see a lot of people walking around carrying large red 3-ring notebooks under their arms, chances are Bill Gothard is in town with a six-day Institute in Basic Youth Conflicts. To be precise, the notebook is eleven and one-half inches wide, ten and one-half inches high, and two and one-fourth inches thick. The cover carries the title, *Institute in Basic Youth Conflicts*, with a descriptive line in smaller type, "Research in Principles of Life." At the bottom of the cover is an emblem of the world and the line, "Giving the World a 'New' Approach to Life!"

It's a loose-leaf book so that it can grow, and every night of the Institute it does grow. At mid-point during the three hour lecture, there is a twenty-minute break during which time everyone gets additional material to put into the book. Incidentally, there is no way you can receive this syllabus except by registering for the seminar. And if you think you'd like to slip away an extra copy to a friend who could really use one, forget it. This book is intended only for the use of those who go through the whole program.

During the week there will be twelve times when portions of the book are distributed. In the front of the book is a little card that lists all twelve times and the name of the material to be distributed then. When you receive yours, that card will be checked off, so you can't go back and get a second copy.

Titles of the materials you will get each day are as follows:

> Monday—Acceptance of Self
> Tuesday—Communication Breakdown
> Wednesday—Clear Conscience, Part One
> Clear Conscience, Part Two
> Thursday—Turning Bitterness to Forgiveness
> Yielding Rights, Transforming Irritations
> Friday—Moral Freedom, Success (purpose),
> Successful Living
> Saturday—Life in a New Dimension, Friendship,
> Successful Dating Patterns.

By the end of the week you'll have nearly 200 pages in your book. The reason the book is loose-leaf is that it can be enlarged. The syllabus says of itself that it "is intended to be 'open ended.' There are many more truths from the inexhaustible pages of scripture which can be added. We encourage you to join us in the deeply rewarding process of doing this." Alumni can bring this same book with them year after year, and the material used at each seminar is essentially the same. There are some changes and elaborations, however, from year to year, so you can constantly keep your book updated.

Ten colored tabs divide the book into sections: self-image; family; conscience; rights; freedom; success; purpose; friends; dating; commitment.

The pages contain diagrams, outlines, charts to be filled in during the lectures, blank space for taking notes. Although Gothard does not follow the notebook precisely page after page in his lectures, the general outline of his lectures is similar to the notebook, and when you come back next year, you can follow along again and recognize that you have been some of these places before.

The red book, plus the notes you take at the seminar, do indeed become a handbook to help remind you of the basics. On its page of instructions on how the book is to be used, it says, "This syllabus is only an incomplete supplement to the 32 hours of lectures, diagrams and charts which make up the basic seminar. The syllabus is designed to be studied along with the many pages of notes which are to be written during the seminar. The purpose of both the seminar and this syllabus is to encourage a much deeper study and application of scripture."

This book is for the basic seminar. There is also an advanced seminar and a minister's manual. We'll say more about that later. The size and comprehensiveness of the red book is impressive. In fact, a quick glance through the book can be overwhelming.

For instance, there are headings like these:
- 6 areas of basic youth conflicts
- 8 qualities essential for success
- 4 levels of conflict
- 3 root problems
- 4 basic steps to spiritual maturity
- 6 ultimate goals of the seminar ministry
- 8 visible symptoms of abnormal social development together with internal conflicts and correlated insights
- 16 rationalizations hindering a clear conscience
- 4 right approaches for gaining a clear conscience
- 5 wrong approaches for gaining a clear conscience
- 8 cautions for gaining a clear conscience
- 6 problems in gaining forgiveness
- 4 steps in removing bitterness
- 4 steps in yielding personal rights
- 3 major sources of irritation
- 3 steps in transforming irritation

    6 steps in understanding forgiveness
    6 steps in narrowing the scope of our lives
    6 steps in widening the scope of our influence
    6 visible symptoms of moral conflict
    6 steps of development of lasciviousness
    5 ways of responding incorrectly to guilt
    6 steps to achieve moral freedom
    5 basic steps toward becoming a "whole person"
    4 basic principles of the structure of our inner
         personality
    6 principles of eternal life
    3 principles of life on how to rebuild your thought
         structures
    2 principles on how to refocus your emotions
    2 principles on how to redirect your life goals
    5 principles on how to get started in successful
         living
    8 callings to a purpose in life
    8 reasons for fasting
    4 discerning levels of friendships
    3 steps for self-acceptance
    3 prerequisites for successful dating
  15 scriptures for discerning genuine love
    4 ways for clarifying my relationship with God
    6 evidences of a spiritual dimension in life
    5 phases of a meaningful exchange with God
    5 basic hindrances to a "total exchange"
    6 steps in detecting reaction to truth

One response to this type of approach can be "How well organized!" It is an impressive pulling together of information in a convenient form that lends itself well to study. And one is able to understand quite readily why it is necessary to have 32 hours of lectures to explain the system.

On the other hand such a listing of 227 steps, principles, ways, phases, areas, etc. can easily cause one to ask, "Is the Christian life really that complicated? What, for instance, if I remember only five evidences of a spiritual dimension in life rather than the six that the handbook lists?" All of these principles listed in the nearly 200 pages of the notebook, by the way, are supported by more than 400 Bible passages.

The Distinction Between Principles and Rules

Gothard does however make a distinction between principles and rules. The red book is sub-titled "Research in *Principles* in Life." Young people would never buy this approach if it were just a bunch of rules, he says. He explains the difference between principles and rules in the following way:

Past generations have had principles to guide their lives, and although the principles themselves were inflexible they could be expressed in a number of rules that were somewhat flexible. The problem was that what they passed down to the next generation were not the principles but the rules.

Furthermore, the children and grandchildren saw that their elders were often not living by the same rules that they were passing on to their children. What the young people today need to learn all over again are some of the basic principles of life and then they can write their own rules.

"In fact," Gothard insists, "the young people themselves will write far more rigid rules for themselves—once they understand the principles—than their elders would write for them."

What is lacking today, he says, is an understanding of basics. You can't understand the individual parts until you understand the whole, he says. That's why he makes no effort to get his story told in the papers. "We haven't wanted stories in the papers because we think bits and pieces of our message will be reported, and the readers will not understand what it is we are saying. We feel we have to give a person a completely new frame of reference for his thoughts. Once he has that, then he can put into it all the information he already has."

That's also why Gothard urges those who attend the seminar not to discuss the content of the red book with outsiders. You really need the full week of concentrated attention to "put things together," he insists. Undoubtedly that's also why the presentation is in lecture form and not in discussion. Principles are not arrived at by consensus or majority vote. They are handed down by God in the Bible. Our job is to find them. And to find them takes the discipline of Bible study, which is then passed on to other people.

Gothard credits his staff for having helped him obtain many insights. Other insights he has gained by personal Bible study, prayer, and fasting. He encourages group Bible study as well as personal Bible study, but a five to twenty thousand audience could not be broken down into "buzz groups" or discussion periods. The Spirit's mode of operation here is through lecture—32 hours of it.

Many Students Repeat the Course

One may be tempted to ask why people come back year after year if the lectures are largely the same, but repetition has always been a good principle for learning. "It means so much more to me the second and third time," is a common expression you hear among alumni. Most recent estimates are that from 40 to 60% of those attending the seminars are doing so for the second, third, or more time. If a periodic review is in order to help you brush up on your grammar, why should it be so surprising that a tool that would help people "brush up" on the principles of living should be in such demand?

Each time a seminar is attended, Gothard says, different areas of personal need usually stand out. Steps of action in these areas should be worked on first. In preparation for this, a time of personal study in the scriptures should be engaged in. The syllabus and lecture notes may become useful in suggesting areas of scripture to study.

It is not the purpose of this book to duplicate the contents of the seminar notebook. Instead we shall attempt to give an overview of four major areas that, to our mind form the clusters around which the whole concept of the Institute in Basic Youth Conflicts revolves.

Gothard himself might not have chosen these four. In fact, my selection of four may be the very reason he is so hesitant about having anyone except himself—or someone closely supervised by him—write a book. He may be fearful that some of the more important principles will be left out.

One could make a different selection, or even take six or eight, but I think the following four—not necessarily in this order of importance—are illustrative of the basic thrust of the Institute in Basic Youth Conflicts:

> The chain of command
> Spirit, Soul and Body
> Dating, marriage, family
> 12 steps to moral purity

But before I treat these areas, I feel it is necessary to talk about Gothard's views on scripture and the nature of God, for these are the foundations on which he builds his system.

46–GOTHARD

Chapter 4

GOTHARD'S USE OF SCRIPTURE

A Bible-Based Seminar

How could any Christian possibly find fault with a program that is so thoroughly Bible-based as is the Institute in Basic Youth Conflicts? Should there not indeed be joy over the fact that literally hundreds of thousands of people flock to the seminars conducted by Bill Gothard? Many of them testify that it is precisely because it is so Bible-based that they are attracted to it. In fact, they say, that for the first time the Bible has made sense to them. They have always had the feeling that the Bible not only is the Word of God but that it is important for them, and they have even had guilt feelings that they didn't understand it properly. Bill Gothard has helped them to see that the Bible is a very practical, everyday book, one that is meant to apply to the daily problems of life.

In the 187 pages of the syllabus that every registrant to the seminar gets, there are more than 480 references to Bible passages, either a reference to them or a quotation of part of a verse or whole verses. David R. Bryen, who wrote a master's thesis on "An Evaluation of the Theological, Hermeneutical and Psychological Assumptions of the Institute in Basic Youth Conflicts," observes:

"It appears from superficial observation that the Bible is the central input factor for the entire seminar. Every concept is presented as coming from the Bible. The insights offered are presented as Biblical insights, the principles are presented as Biblical principles.... Many people are impressed by what they consider to be Gothard's unique, fresh, and practical insights into interpreting and applying Biblical truth."

New Attention to the Wisdom Literature

Not only are the seminars filled with scripture, but they also focus attention on those portions of the Bible known as Wisdom Literature—Proverbs, Psalms, Ecclesiastes, the Sermon on the Mount, and practical portions of Paul's letters. Richard Beckmen, a clergyman of The American Lutheran Church and a professional worker with youth credits Gothard for drawing attention to this one vast area of the Bible seldom used in today's mainline churches.

Says Beckmen, "The wisdom tradition is a major strain of Biblical thought. However, separated out from the context of Exodus-covenant-incarnation-crucifixion as a major theme, it creates a dangerous situation. A discipling process that focuses strictly on the wisdom tradition usually ends up being legalistic in its expression and experience. On the other hand, a discipling process that does not take seriously the dilemma of deciding upon personal action and the necessity of guidance for the individual creates a frustrated disciple."

In other words, Beckmen is arguing that perhaps precisely because the mainline churches have largely overlooked the value of this wisdom literature in the Bible, a vacuum has been left that Bill Gothard is filling. "His primary focus on scripture and directions toward meditation clearly respond to a need in the church," says Beckmen. "How does the modern Christian interiorize the scriptures and allow the truth that is in them to become a source of strength and direction? Gothard goes beyond memorization (although he advocates this strongly) to provide a significant process for persons to get into scripture."

The people evidently are finding Gothard's approach useful to them. In an era when general morality is at a low ebb, he is providing clues for establishing a clear Biblical base for Christian thought and action. What's more, people are convinced it will work. Gothard is able to supply them with example after example as evidence of that fact.

Why not then let it go at that? Even if one could find some scholarly and technical flaws in some of Gothard's presentations, isn't there evidence that an overwhelming number of people have found his approach useful, and testify to the fact that they have been driven back into the scriptures by his approach?

The accusation that Gothard misuses scripture may be the hardest one of all to understand by those who find his seminars so exciting. They are convinced that that is the very strength of his programs. For him the scripture has the answer to all of life's problems. And isn't that really what we all believe!

The Purpose of Scripture

Even though I agree with Gothard that in scripture we can find the answers to life's problems, I find myself in great disagreement about the actual methods by which those answers are obtained from the Bible. Probably in the majority of instances our conclusions would be the same, even though our ways of reaching them may differ. But at some very crucial points where our conclusions disagree, I feel that the tension is not semantic but based on a fundamental difference in how we interpret scripture.

One of the problems in dealing with this issue of the proper use of the Bible is that it is so close to the very heart and soul of everything that is Christian that it is difficult if not impossible to view it objectively, dispassionately, and unemotionally. Conservative Christians are so imbued with the fact that the Bible is the Word of God that even to raise questions of how it came into being raises a warning flag. We have all heard of people who through false teachings have sought to destroy faith in the Bible. Many of them, however, may indeed not have wanted to do that at all, but have merely raised questions in order to get a better understanding of the Bible. But the necessity of preserving the Bible as the Word of God is so inbred in many of us that every question, no matter how well intentioned, raises suspicions in almost knee-jerk fashion.

The word "inerrant" becomes a key word in a discussion of how we understand the Bible to be God's Word. There are essentially two schools of thought trying to explain the nature of God's communication to man. One group holds that when the Bible speaks about those things that pertain to our salvation, then it is without error. But since the Bible was not intended as a textbook in science or geography, and was in fact written in a day when the scientific world view held that the earth was flat, we should not insist that it is also without error in scientific matters. Furthermore, some of the writings of the Bible are in the form of poetry and parable and need not be taken literally. For instance, the point of the Jonah story is not the historical fact whether a man lived in the belly of a big fish for three days and then was regurgitated, or whether God is powerful enough to make a fish big enough to do that and then keep the man alive for three days. The point of the story is what happens to a man when he tries to run away from God.

However, the other school will have none of this kind of reasoning. In fact it considers it dangerous to the faith. For them the whole of the Bible is without error and should be taken literally. If the Jonah story is in question, then how are we to know whether the Easter story is any more true?

Furthermore, isn't there always the danger that we can water down the Bible, so that whenever we find something we would rather not believe, we can find a way of explaining it away? This is precisely the argument that Gothard uses in attacking those who would explain away his interpretations. For him the Bible is the absolute inerrant Word of God in all its parts and on all topics.

Although the literalistic, inerrant view is simpler to apply, it has serious problems. The most obvious is that the very nature of communication itself is often figurative and heavily dependent on the listener. What cause have we to believe that God in communicating Himself to man would confine Himself to only literal statements?

We must also confront the fact that the Bible was written in a culture totally different from ours. That does not mean it has no meaning for us. Indeed it does have meaning, but to understand it, one must first of all understand what it meant to the people to whom it was originally written. Bible study involves much more than merely learning words, or even meditating on them. One must take into account what they meant the first time they were written.

Another problem is that Gothard treats the Bible as an authority on all sorts of matters merely because it contains some mention of that particular topic.

Recalling my own experience at one of Gothard's seminars, I am reminded of his favorite approach of stating a problem and then asking, "You know what the answer is?" Then he would state a scripture passage that gave the answer. The Bible is essentially an answer book, a verse here to answer this problem, a verse there to answer that problem, so that the more scripture passages you can learn the more problems in life you can answer. Gothard likes to challenge people to come up with a problem for which he can't quote a Bible passage as an answer.

It is interesting to hear all the principles that Gothard finds in the Bible, not least of which are principles that would make one successful in business. He tells, for instance, of how by following Biblical principles his organization saved $10,000 on a printing bill and $25,000 on a construction bill. "That's because we did it according to principles outlined in the Bible," he said.

In giving the details of these instances, he says that the traditional, business way of deciding on where to get a contract is to get three bids and then take the lowest bid. But the Bible suggests a different way. When King Solomon made plans to build the temple and went to Hiram to get cedars from Lebanon, he did not get a quotation from him. Solomon told Hiram what he would pay and then he sent his own workers to work along side those of Hiram.

"We decided to follow a similar procedure," he said. "We did our own estimating as to what material and labor costs would be. We were aware that a company needs profits, so we simply found out what percentage of a job companies generally used as a mark-up for profit. We added that in and then we approached a reputable company and said we will give you so much. They took our offer, and it saved us $10,000 from what would ordinarily have been the lowest bid on one occasion, and $25,000 on another occasion. From now on we're going to do all of our business according to Biblical principles."

Gothard told the audience at the Detroit seminar that a number of business firms are currently experimenting by doing all of their transactions according to Biblical principles, and he is convinced that the result will be that these companies will be more successful, because the Bible says that when you follow God's way you will prosper in everything you do, even in your business transactions.

My argument with Gothard is not that the illustrations he uses were not a practice of good business that everyone ought to follow or that everyone ought not to follow the best kind of business practices that result in the best returns. My argument is that it is *not the purpose of the Bible* to give that kind of information. What does he do, for instance, with the Jubilee Year, when every 50 years all property went back to the original owners?

The genius of the Bible is that while it was written for a particular people, at a particular time in history, with their own cultural and economic patterns, the main message of salvation is translatable for all times no matter what the culture or economic system may be. The Bible was not written to undergird simply a capitalistic system of economics. The principles of the Bible can work under socialism too, but the Bible does not endorse only one kind of economic system.

Or, take his reference to some of the Old Testament cultic rituals, out of which Gothard extracts some principles of medicine. The fifth chapter of Numbers describes a way to test the truthfulness of a wife as to whether or not she has had sexual relations with another man. Again, relying on his illustration of the necessary balance between the body and soul and spirit, he says that any kind of conscience problem will reflect itself in a chemical imbalance in the body. According to Hebrew ritual, a wife who is being interrogated for this alleged offense is to present herself to the priest who will make her drink holy water mixed with dust from the ground. If she is innocent, her chemical balance will be in order, and she will suffer no ill consequences, but if she is guilty, the chemical imbalance of her body will be such that her body will swell. Medical science does indeed support the finding that there is a delicate chemical balance in the body that is affected by emotions, not because that is a teaching of the Bible—because the Bible is not a textbook on science or medicine—but because the findings of science are also gifts and revelations of God.

Distorting Scripture to Support One's Preconceptions

It is possible to make extensive use of the Bible, to quote it with extreme frequency as Gothard does, and still use it in a way that many other people, equally convinced that the Bible is the Word of God, think is a misuse. For

Gothard, the Bible is fundamentally a book of God-given *principles*.

In an introductory brochure, Gothard says: "This seminar is the result of 15 years of youth work. It is based on the fact that there are underlying *principles* of life set forth in scriptures and that there is a clear relationship between violations of these principles and the conflicts that both youth and adults are facing today."

One of the problems with this kind of interpretation of scripture is that it is very heavily dependent upon cause and effect relationships. When we see an effect, we look for a cause. There is nothing wrong with that except that when we have observed certain things happening in life, we are then prone to look for those things in scripture that point to the effect we have just seen, and become blind to other things that the scripture might be trying to tell us.

Bryen reports having had a conversation with Gothard during which he made a casual connection between the mild winter America was having at that time and the military aid America had given to the nation of Israel. The verse Gothard cited to support his view was Genesis 12:13, "And I will bless those who bless you, and the one who curses you I will curse." My contention is that this is not what that verse meant when it was first spoken, and for us with the benefit of hindsight to read interpretations of this kind into the Bible has some dangerous implications—as will be pointed out later.

Illustrations of this type are numerous throughout the seminar. The pattern is that principles are discovered either through the observation of life or study of scripture, and then the Bible is searched for *additional* places where that principle is illustrated or supported. Those portions of the Bible that might indeed go contrary to this principle are neatly overlooked.

One of the very obvious considerations in Gothard's use of the Bible, says Bryen, is the tendency that his "interpretations are governed more by his personal experiences than he cares to admit." Bible scholars point out the danger of failing to appreciate the degree to which the outcome of the interpretation is due to prior convictions.

Since Gothard does seemingly fail to consider his own assumptions as factors in the final interpretation of scripture, it is not surprising to find many cases of misinterpreted data. An example of this kind of interpretation is given by R. T. Coote, who reported in *Eternity* magazine on one of Gothard's seminars. Coote, in an article generally favorable toward Gothard, describes a particularly novel interpretation that he gives of the book of Job, chapters 1, 21, 29, 30, and 31.

"Against the clear Biblical statement that Job was a righteous man and that he suffered because of no sin of his own," Coote says, "Gothard claims: 1) Job was overcommitted to Christian work and good deeds; 2) this led to his neglecting the family; 3) therefore, his sons became embittered against God and cursed Him at their parties; 4) this was the reason Job wasn't invited to join them; 5) Job had a wrong attitude toward the man-in-the-street. Instead of desiring to have a spiritual ministry in the lives of other men he evaluated them only in terms of their usefulness to his 'organization,' working with his herds."

Commenting on this, Bryen observes: "Here, concern for balance in ministry and work responsibilities cause Gothard to make Job say what is needed at the moment rather than extracting the actual meaning from the text . . . . Gothard's hidden interpretive context, demanding cause and effect principles from the Bible, causes him only to see what his interpretive context demands that he see."

It is not an overstatement to say that this kind of use of scripture has some distinct dangers connected with it. A proper understanding of the Bible does not come about by picking out some "principle" statements that support either preconceived ideas or ideas that may indeed have come from the Bible itself but that need to be enlightened by exposure to the whole of scripture.

I am also aware that slaveholders in the 1800's found statements in the Bible that supported their principle of slavery. The whites in South Africa today insist that the reason they are treating the blacks as second class citizens or worse is that they are convinced there are statements in the Bible that support their view.

One final example should be sufficient to warn the reader against distorting scriptures to support a preconception. In one of his lectures I heard Gothard say:

"There are those who say, 'What's wrong with drinking a little wine? Doesn't the Bible say that Jesus himself made wine?' It is inconceivable that Jesus made wine. Wine comes about through a process of decomposition. Decomposition is a part of death, and Jesus was the exact opposite of death. He is life himself. It is inconceivable that Jesus could be party to something that involved death. It is absolutely inconceivable that Jesus made wine." It should be obvious to the reader that when scripture is treated like this, it can be made to say anything.

I am not the only one who has problems with some of Gothard's interpretation of scripture. Bryen, who has already been quoted several times, says: "Gothard places a system of belief over his study and meditation so that only truth compatible with his presuppositions comes into focus. With the proof texts and examples from life to validate his presuppositions, the faith in his assumptions becomes stronger and stronger. By selecting this kind of selective interpretation the Institute in Basic Youth Conflicts loses the completeness of scripture's balance. This loss of balance is devastating to the Bible's message."

Another writer says, "Gothard's system is inadequate because it is modified by his presuppositions, and is only large enough to deal with data compatible with his presuppositions. The problem is more than simply isolated examples of interpretative error; it's a faulty *system* of interpretation. The criticisms come from recurrent disregard for context, disregard for culture, magical manipulation and quotation of the Bible, severely limiting the various perspectives of Scripture, and textual twisting to fit presumed principles.

"The system is faulty because it undercuts the authenticity of Scripture. Scripture is 'used' to fit into the Basic Youth Conflicts system, but in so doing it has become subservient to the principles of the seminar. The Bible no longer has the power to correct the system, but it is used as an authoritarian tool to appeal for application of the principles."

Although not referring specifically to Gothard and his Institute, some of the comments made by J. D. Smart in his book *The Strange Silence Of The Bible In The Church* is *apropos* to the method of Bible interpretation used at the seminars:

"(There) are many instances of deeply earnest people who read their Bibles in a context which, to our mind, produces a grossly distorted gospel. There is no mystery about the forces that have shaped their interpretative context for them. They are the products of an aggressive capitalist economy with its individualistic philosophy of life, or of a society that has permitted the lines of racial discrimination to harden into walls. Their way of reading Scripture has been subtly adapted to prevent any collision between what they hear in Scripture and the order to society that they prefer."

The big question still remains—why are hundreds of thousands of well-meaning Christians impressed with the Gothard seminars, and convinced of their worth largely because they are so completely based on scripture? And, is our criticism of Gothard's Biblical interpretation valid enough that a note of danger needs to be sounded?

Obviously, people will continue to flock to the seminars and be changed for the good. And it may well be that the kind of Bible studies conducted in traditional churches are not complete either. Maybe they need to capture a new vision of the wisdom literature in the Bible and the fact that these portions in the Bible do speak to everyday life.

At the same time, however, our personal evaluation of Gothard's approach convinces us that at very best it's truncated.

An Alternative

But do I have an alternative to offer? Is there another interpretation of the Bible—apart from the answer-book and principles of life approach—that is more useful? Perhaps no one approach to the Bible is all-inclusive, and one should never expect one vehicle to carry the whole freight. Without my suggesting that it is either the best or the only way of interpreting scripture, let me share what for me is a meaningful way of looking at the Bible.

I was eight years old when the Bible became excitingly real for me. Not that I hadn't been aware of it before. We had it in our home. It was a big black book, written in German, and either my father or mother read from it during morning and evening family devotions.

Our church had no Sunday School at the time. We had three months of Bible school every summer—from 9 o'clock in the morning till 4 o'clock in the afternoon. Every youngster from the congregation attended that school for five years, starting in the summer after his second year in the public school. (Public school was of eight months duration at that time.) I had become an avid reader during my first few years in public school, and during my second grade I found a book in the school library that was engagingly fascinating.

It told the story of a lad by the name of David who fought with and killed Goliath, a giant. Another man, Daniel, spent a night in the lion's den. And then there were those three men with the unbelievable names of Shadrach, Mishak, and Abednego, who spent a night in a fiery furnace and walked out unscathed. Even the best of cowboy stories couldn't compare with them in excitement. Then I went to our summer church school. A high priority was given to Bible stories. I still remember my surprise and excitement when I heard these same stories that I had read in that book at the public school library and discovered that they were *Bible stories.*

I'll always be glad that I was introduced to the Bible in this way, as an exciting book about a God who dealt with real people in an exciting way, people with joys and sorrow, and passions and anger. The Bible is a story of real life, of people who get angry at God but who also experience the forgiveness and acceptance of God.

Nowhere does the Bible allow any latitude for evil, but it is filled with forgiveness for those who have fallen. When I read the story of the Prodigal Son, the thing that captivates me is the amazing love that God has for us, not the principles of what happens to one who wastes his substance in riotous living. I find very little in abstract life principles, but much in relationships.

The joy of Bible study is not to try to find all the principles of right living for fear that I might forget some of them, but rather to get acquainted with God, and with a live person, Jesus Christ, as well as with a host of other interesting characters who are described in their encounters with God.

60–GOTHARD

Chapter 5

WHAT KIND OF A GOD?

Gothard's View of God

While Gothard has no one period during his week's seminar that is devoted to a lecture on the doctrine of God, there are some assumptions about God that underlie and penetrate every lecture. It would be helpful for us to gather together all of those assumptions in an attempt to help us understand what is Gothard's view of God upon which he has built his principles of living.

Gothard's theology most closely resembles that of the Reformed tradition, in which one of the key concepts is the *sovereignty* of God. God is like an absolute monarch, an undisputed master, who has absolute wisdom and knows everything that is going on in the world.

God is exacting in His demand of perfect obedience to His commands. Although He is a God of love, He is not a God who can be dealt with lightly. He is not one whom we can engage in a discussion and persuade that perhaps He ought not to be quite so rigid.

One feels that the kind of God whom we can slap on the shoulder and with whom we can enjoy a casual if not cavalier relationship is not capable of dealing with the problems of our age. In fact, that seems why we have an age of problems: too much indecisiveness, laxity, permissiveness. We have an inborn feeling that there needs to be someone in control who can have the final word. The kind of God who can still storms is one who will not be pushed around.

It's much easier these days to believe in a God who makes some stringent demands. Perhaps it is an indication of our maturity that we are no longer willing to settle for a God who bends with the fads of the day. The very fact that people by the hundreds of thousands are sitting through hours of lectures laced with this kind of picture of God ought to serve as an example to those churches and groups—not growing as rapidly—who still think that people will not respond to anything that portrays the kind of God Gothard describes.

Man's Knowledge of God

God's revelation of Himself is not by means of propositions, but through His various dealings with mankind. Sometimes that revelation is regarded as a paradox. For example, He is a God of justice, who—if He is to remain God—must insist that all laws be kept. But He is also a God of mercy, who loves the sinner at the same time that He abhors the sin. But human beings are so constituted that they find it difficult to deal with ambiguity. We are much more comfortable when every paradox can be resolved, because we want to be able to understand and explain what we experience.

What is essentially at stake is reason versus faith—reason being the insistence on something that *can be seen* or that satisfies rational explanation, as over against faith, which is established on trust not dependent on what can be seen or explained. Our problem is that we have only human minds and a human language with which to understand and articulate divine realities, and there is always a gap between the two. Human analogies are helpful, but they never tell the whole story. They always leave unanswered questions. Problems arise when we insist that the whole of divine reality must submit to human explanation.

Luther used to speak of the *Deus Abscunditus*, "the hidden God" who never totally reveals Himself. Human reason would say that the more we know about this God the less hidden He becomes. The law of pure arithmetic is at work. If originally He was 100% unknown, and we learned about 30% of Him, then He should be only 70% unknown. But human reason doesn't apply in working with divine realities. Rather the more we know about Him the greater we stand in awe of the great mysteries of God, and the more humble we become.

Robert McAfee Brown in his book, *Frontiers for the Church Today*, says it this way: "The reason for invoking a sense of mystery is not to offer a description of 'things we don't yet understand,' but rather to describe the way we handle the things we do understand.... Even in a world of computers, the arts continue. People give expression to the many dimensions of their existence in ways that are not reducible to predictable formulas or data-gathering processes or the amount of a glandular secretion. It is important that a sense of wonder continue to intrude into and inform all cultures and all societies, no matter how much people try to build fences against it."

The Problem of Evil

Any person who places a strong emphasis on the sovereignty of God must sooner or later speak to the problem of evil.

This problem basically reduces the question: "If God foresaw everything that was going to happen, and if He allowed it to happen, then—since He is the omnipotent, sovereign God—He must also have *intended* it to happen. But if He intended it to happen and allowed it to happen, is He then also the cause of everything that happens, *even sin?*"

The traditional way to answer this question is to distinguish between *causing* something to happen and *allowing* it to happen, thus freeing God from the charge of being the cause of evil. But when Gothard maintains absolute sovereignty so strongly it is difficult to see how he can avoid calling God the author of evil, for if God has "foreordained whatsoever comes to pass," evil must be included in "whatsoever."

Attitude Toward Struggles

Gothard holds that since God has caused or allowed everything to happen that does happen, it is our duty to accept our lot without complaining. And since He is also a God of love, He has everyone's best interest at heart. Therefore because our own vision is always incomplete we must withhold judgment at moments of pain. God has a purpose in mind with the pain that is being inflicted on us.

Two of Gothard's favorite analogies in this connection are the unfinished painting and the diamond being polished. If we complain because of the lot that has befallen us in life, we need to be reminded that the picture isn't completed yet. Give God some more time and we too will be a beautiful picture.

The diamond, the most exquisite and valuable of all precious stones, achieves greater exquisiteness with long and expert polishing with an abrasive. God wants us to be a diamond. He achieves that by polishing us, much of it perhaps painful, but it is for our greater glory as well as His. He uses other people, chiefly our parents and those in authority over us, as the stone cutter's chisel to give us the characteristics of a diamond.

Gothard sees "the Christian teen-ager as a 'diamond in the rough.' God's purpose, then, is to use parents as His tools, guided by His hands, in chipping away the rough edges of each life so that the true reflection of Christ can be seen from every angle."

The Undergraduate Gothard

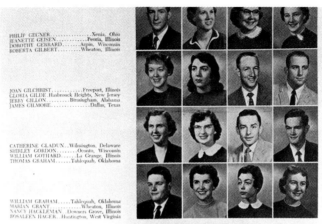

PHILIP GEGNER..............Xenia, Ohio
JEANETTE GEISEN...........Peoria, Illinois
DOROTHY GERRARD.......Arpin, Wisconsin
ROBERTA GILBERT.........Wheaton, Illinois

JOAN GILCHRIST............Freeport, Illinois
GLORIA GILDE.Hasbrouck Heights, New Jersey
JERRY GILLON..........Birmingham, Alabama
JAMES GILMORE...............Dallas, Texas

CATHERINE GLADUN..Wilmington, Delaware
SHIRLEY GORDON........Oconto, Wisconsin
WILLIAM GOTHARD......La Grange, Illinois
THOMAS GRAHAM......Tahlequah, Oklahoma

WILLIAM GRAHAM.....Tahlequah, Oklahoma
MARIAN GRANT...........Wheaton, Illinois
NANCY HACKLEMAN .Downers Grove, Illinois
ROSALEEN HAGER. Huntington, West Virginia

———— CLASS OF 1957 ————

AVA HALSEY...............Olivet, Michigan
DONALD HAMMAN..French Equatorial, Africa
LARRY HAMMERBERG,
                    McKeesport, Pennsylvania
GIL HAMON................Hillside, Illinois

Bill Gothard's present, and well known, reluctance to be photographed appears at a relatively early point in his life. In 1956 as a junior at Wheaton College in Wheaton, Illinois, his picture appears just once in the *Tower 56* yearbook.

Institute Headquarters

The headquarters of the Institute in Basic Youth Conflicts is located on North Adams Street in the Chicago suburb of Hinsdale, Illinois. Below: entrance to the Institute headquarters. Upper right: Visitors entrance. Lower right: View of Institute offices.

In June, 1972, thousands of people packed the Long
Beach Arena in California, for an Institute in Basic
Youth Conflicts.

The Seminar

When an Institute in Basic Youth Conflicts is held in a major city, usually the largest auditorium in that city is reserved for the week. During the first week in August, 1976, the Arie Crown Theater in Chicago's famous convention center, McCormick Place, was the site of the Institute. When the Institute is in session, only an occasional staff member may be found outside the auditorium. Right, above. The scene is different as the seminar lets out. Below.

The Big Red Book

Right: The Institute notebook available only to people attending the seminar. Below: The notebook contains much highly organized information, charts, illustrations, scripture references, all designed to supplement and complete the daily lectures.

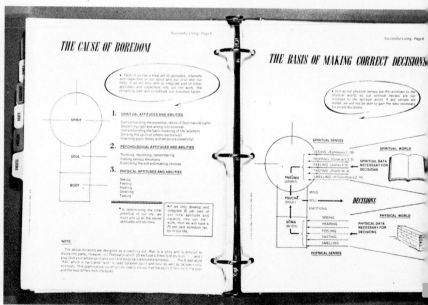

And isn't it true that the formation of the beautiful is often accompanied by pain? The irritation of the grain of sand in the oyster results in the production of a pearl. Solid and strong character is often formed through the struggle against opposition.

There are many scripture illustrations, and Gothard uses them to strengthen his point. Joseph is sold by his brothers as a slave into Egypt. It was undoubtedly a traumatic experience. But Joseph is able to say later to his brothers, "You meant it unto me for evil, but God meant it unto good." There is the well-known story of Paul and his "thorn in the flesh." Three times Paul prayed that the Lord might take it away from him, but it stayed, and became a means of growth. Paul thanked God for it.

History is replete with similar instances. Pain is often the instrument of and the road to growth. Nothing important comes easily. Gothard takes that principle so seriously that absolutely everything that happens to a person must be seen in that light. The corollary then is that people must learn to praise God for the misfortunes in life, for they can be assured that God had a good purpose for them.

However, in this connection one wonders how seriously to take Gothard's insistence that the Christian must not balk at his lot; for Gothard's whole Institute is based on the assumption that there is something wrong with people that needs to be changed.

An Alternative

I find serious problems with Gothard's model of God as a sovereign ruler. Not that it is incorrect, but that it is inadequate to do justice to the full range of information given to us about God in the Bible.

There is too much emphasis on unquestioning obedience, which suggests that God is more interested in rules than in a relationship with His people. J. D. Carter, writing in *Journal of Psychology and Theology*, says, "Since the

Bible is used as a book of rules, the spontaneity, joy, freedom and liberty which exist in Christ are absent. God is presented as an impersonal deity instead of a loving father. Gothard's system has a morality of law and legalism rather than the love and grace morality so prevalent in the New Testament."

There is too much acquiescence to whatever happens as being God's will. P. R. Keating, in an article on Gothard appearing in *Eternity* magazine, says, "One overall seminar theme emerges with nagging implications. This is the total quiescent acceptance of what is, a nirvana of spirit that acquiesces unquestioningly to God's will. There is no suggestion of a Davidic or Abrahamic arguing with God. Who was it that insistently argued for the life of Sodom? Which psalmist wondered if God was going to be embarrassed by what people might think? Didn't Jesus question whether the cross was the only way? Should we not question deeply the tragedy and inequity in our world and social system? Should we for generations have raised no question about our attitude toward those of another race? Hasn't it been those who have been enraged by disease or retardation or social injustice or pollution and the like that have brought correctives? We must find a way to live with the paradox of seeing what is our lot as God's will, while at the same time struggling to subdue the forces of evil that plague our world."

The above-mentioned problems, and others as well, would be greatly minimized by substituting the model of God as Person, a model which permeates the writings of C.S. Lewis.

Briefly stated, the view is that God can best be understood as a person, unique in the fact that He is omnipotent, omniscient and all good. Because He desired a loving relationship with other persons, He created man. However, in order for that relationship to be meaningful, God had to allow man the freedom to choose it or to reject it. When God made man a free moral person, He thereby chose to limit His own sovereignty. This self-limitation opened up the possibility for both a creative loving relationship and a destructive alienated relationship. God obviously felt that the self-limitation was worth the risk in order to realize the good of love between Himself and men.

In the revelation of moral laws in scripture, we should note that their summation is in loving God and one's neighbor, so that the assumption is that loving relationships are to take priority over rules and regulation. Furthermore, one gets the impression that when we suffer the consequences of our sins, God is less willing to point the accusing finger than He is to grieve over the love lost.

A further advantage of using the model of God as Person is that we need not be intimidated by all the talk about God as mysterious and beyond our full understanding. This is true of persons in general. At no point in any relationship can we say, "I have exhausted all there is to know about you." This is because persons cannot be reduced to an objective list of qualities; there is always a remainder. This is true of God to an even greater extent.

The final area that the person model sheds light on is the traditional dichotomy between faith and reason. Those who make this distinction hold that faith is essential whether we have sufficient reasons for believing or not; and that human reason is suspect because man sinfully refuses to believe unless he can know all about God first. This dichotomy fails to take into account that in any personal relationship we come to trust a person as we learn more about him. There is a point (far short of full knowledge) where we say, "I believe I have enough evidence to trust that person." Therefore, we need not speak of reason vs. faith, but reason able to lead men to faith.

Because of the above considerations, I believe that the model of God as Loving Person offers a more adequate and comprehensive picture than the model of God as Sovereign Ruler.

Chapter 6

THE CHAIN OF COMMAND

The Concept of Authority

Few things are so contrary to prevailing cultural attitudes, so hotly debated—and perhaps also misunderstood—and yet so basic to the whole concept of the Institute in Basic Youth Conflicts as the chain of command. That this movement should become so strong at the same time that the women's liberation movement is growing is something of an anomaly.

Very simply, the chain of command means that everyone is under authority, and God deals with people through these channels of authority. God, of course, is the chief authority, and He works through four basic structures: family, government, church, and business.

In the family the chain of command places the father at the top, then the mother, and then the children. In government, the citizens are under the authority of local officials, who are under the authority of national leaders. In the church, the authority flows from the church leaders down to church members. And in business, the chain of command is from employer to employees.

Gothard is convinced that this is God's plan. And even those of us who may not agree with it might do well to ponder a little more deeply just what is at stake here. Gothard is getting at the roots of the very deep problem in American culture of how to deal with the whole concept of authority.

We, by nature, simply rebel against the fact that we cannot be totally independent. The essence of the fall into sin is the desire on the part of Adam and Eve to be as God, that is to be totally independent and not answerable to anyone. We prefer to go our way, without having to consult the wishes of someone else. The fact is that according to Genesis 3 God did *not* give unlimited freedom to Adam and Eve. He said you can eat of all the trees in the garden *except one*. You may *not eat* of the tree of the knowledge of good and evil, for the day you eat of it you will die. In other words, God was exercising authority. This was not something that could be decided by popular vote. Some laws God declares by pure fiat, simply because He is God. That is the basis of authority. Since the very essence of sin is a rejection of authority, it behooves us to give ear to people such as Gothard who call attention to this basic relationship between God and His people, and to insist that this is also a *principle* basic to all relationships, even though this goes contrary to most of popular human thought today.

The four structures of human society as described by Gothard—family, government, church, and business—all must operate with an understanding of what authority means, and what happens when authority is undermined. Since there are many who are convinced that one of the major problems of society today is the breakdown of authority, it is not surprising that Gothard should have such a following. People have a gut level feeling that there needs to be a return to authority.

Scriptural Support for Authority

Gothard has ample scripture passages to substantiate

each aspect of the chain of command. For the family author-ity structure there are these:

"Children, obey your parents in all things; for this is well pleasing unto the Lord" *Colossians 3:20.*

"Children, obey your parents in the Lord: for this is right. Honor thy father and mother; which is the first com-mandment with promise; that it may be well with thee, and thou mayest live long on the earth" *Ephesians 6:1-3.*

"My son, keep thy father's commandment, and for-sake not the law of thy mother; bind them continually upon thine heart, and tie them about thy neck" *Proverbs 6:20,21.*

"The eye that mocketh at his father, and despiseth to obey his mother, the ravens of the valley shall pick it out, and the young eagles shall eat it" *Proverbs 30:17.*

"A fool despiseth his father's instruction; but he that regardeth reproof is prudent" *Proverbs 15:5.*

To substantiate the chain of command in the govern-ment structure, Gothard uses these passages:

"Submit yourselves to every ordinance of man for the Lord's sake; whether it be the king, as supreme or unto gov-ernors, as unto them that are sent by him for the punishment of evildoers, and for the praise of them that do well" *I Peter 2:13,14.*

"Let every soul be subject unto the higher powers. For there is no power but of God: the powers that be are ordained of God" *Romans 13:1.*

"For rulers are not a terror to good works, but to the evil . . . for he is the minister of God to thee for good" *Ro-mans 13:3,4.*

"Wherefore ye must needs be subject, not only for wrath, but also for conscience sake" *Romans 13:5.*

"For this cause pay ye tribute also: for they are God's ministers, attending continually upon this very thing. Ren-der therefore to all their dues . . ." *Romans 13:6,7.*

Gothard also points to Bible passages that set church leaders over church members:

"And we beseech you, brethren, to know them which labor among you, and are over you in the Lord, and admonish you: and to esteem them very highly in love for their works sake" *I Thessalonians 5:12,13*.

"Obey them that have rule over you, and submit yourselves: for they watch for your souls, as them that must give account, that they may do it with joy and not with grief: for that is unprofitable for you" *Hebrews 13:17*.

"Let the elders that rule well be counted worthy of double honor, especially them who labor in the word and doctrine ... and the laborer is worthy of his reward" *I Timothy 5:17,18*.

"The elders which are among you I exhort ... Feed the flock of God which is among you, taking the oversight thereof, not by constraint, but willingly; not for filthy lucre, but of a ready mind; neither as being lords over God's heritage, but being ensamples to the flock" *I Peter 5:1-3*.

Gothard lists five scripture passages that establish the chain of command from employer to employee:

"Servants, obey in all things your masters according to the flesh; not with eyeservice, as menpleasers, but in singleness of heart, fearing God" *Colossians 3:22*.

"And whatsoever ye do, do it heartily, as unto the Lord, and not unto men; knowing that of the Lord he shall receive the reward of the inheritance: for ye serve the Lord Christ" *Colossians 3:23,24*.

"Servants be subject to your masters with all fear; not only to the good and gentle, but also to the froward" *I Peter 2:18*.

"Let as many servants as are under the yoke count their own masters worthy of all honor, that the name of God and his doctrine be not blasphemed" *I Timothy 6:1*.

"And they that have believing masters, let them not despise them ... but rather do them service" *I Timothy 6:2*.

Some of these are hard sayings. For instance take I Peter 2:18: "Servants be subject to your masters with all fear; *not only to the good and gentle, but also to the froward."* Not very many union contracts are written on that basis these days. But what do you do if you are a Christian and believe that the Bible is the Word of God? Are you just free to disregard those passages that aren't to your liking? Can you adjust or rewrite the Bible to suit your prejudices?

Heavy Emphasis on the Family

Although all four of these areas are emphasized in the seminar, the heaviest emphasis comes on the chain of command in the family structure. Gothard likes to speak of this through the image of an umbrella. Being under authority, he says, is not like getting under the *domination* of authority. "Authority is like an *'umbrella of protection'* and when we get out from under it, we expose ourselves to unnecessary temptations which are too strong for us to overcome."

Although most of his references are to those under authority, to insist that they indeed remain obedient, he also has some strong words to say to those—particularly fathers—who are in authority, to make sure that their umbrellas aren't leaking, allowing temptations to come through to attack those under them. Gothard says in one of his lectures: "Satan cannot get through to some sons and daughters unless there is a leak in the father's umbrella."

For instance, if a child has a drug problem, Gothard would ask the father, "Do you smoke? Do you drink? If you do, these are leaks in your umbrella through which Satan can come to tempt those under your case. You patch up your umbrella, and you'll be surprised to see the effect it will have on your son or daughter."

The wife is also definitely under the husband's authority umbrella. "Before the fall," says Gothard, "Eve had a different relationship. Satan came directly to Eve instead of through Adam. When the woman was beguiled, God put a restriction on her. ("Thy desire shall be to thy husband, and he shall rule over thee" *Genesis 3:16.*) But this restriction was for her own protection. Now Satan can no longer get through to her unless he goes through the husband."

"I would beg you, I would plead with you to accept this as a valid Christian concept," Gothard told his 8,600 listeners in the Detroit seminar.

And for those who think that this is hopelessly outmoded, Gothard can tell story after convincing story of incidents in which formerly quarreling families achieved a new and happy relationship once they submitted to this structure. He also has a very easy answer for those for whom it has not worked: they just haven't tried it long enough yet.

This pattern is set very strongly at the very beginning of the seminar. On the first night he tells the story of a young Christian lady, in every respect a model of faith. She has accepted Christ as her personal saviour. She is committed to him. She is a faithful student of the Bible—all of the qualities and characteristics that made a good Christian.

She falls in love with a young man with precisely the same characteristics. They pray about their relationship and they decide to get married, convinced that their plans have God's blessing. But the parents of the girl, who are not Christians themselves, object. What does she do? No matter how rational an argument you can give that she should go ahead and get married, the fact is—according to Gothard—that this is not God's way. She must be obedient *always* to her parents.

The only time you are justified in disobeying your parents is if they ask you to do something that is against the command of God. Parents may even be wrong and unreasonable in their stand, but that is not sufficient reason for a child to disobey parents.

To the question, "What if I don't respect the authority over me?" Gothard replies, "It is important that we learn how to distinguish between an authority's position under God and his human personality. We are to reverence his position, although at the same time we may be very aware of personality deficiencies. To say that we reject an authority because we don't respect him would be as much in error as tearing up a speeding ticket because we didn't like the attitude of the arresting officer."

Furthermore, if some parents are unreasonable with their children, this very characteristic may be what God is using to build character in these children. Again, Gothard is able to tell story after story about instances like the young model Christian couple who were convinced it was God's will for them to be married over their parents' objections, and who later found nothing but misery in their life.

In the parent-child relationship, Gothard nowhere suggests that the child should turn into an absolute doormat and allow himself or herself to be walked all over—at least not forever. He does make a good case however for patiently bearing some burdens, with the confidence that God will eventually right all inequities. To illustrate that, he tells this story:

A high school student asked his father if he could stay after school and go to the prayer meeting at the church. The father said he could on the one condition that he come straight home after it was over. The boy did this and on the way home a friend of his picked him up in the car and brought him the rest of the way. He had not disobeyed his father. He had come straight home. But his father was awaiting him on the steps.

"I told you you could go to the prayer meeting and then come straight home. You disobeyed me. You didn't go to the prayer meeting at all. You went out with your friend."

The son assured him that he had indeed gone to the prayer meeting and had come straight home and had merely gotten a ride the last part of the way.

"And now you add a lie to disobedience," the angry father shouted, and took off his belt and whipped the boy. The boy took it all in silence, even though it was a gross injustice.

The next week the father happened to be with the pastor, and the pastor said, "You certainly have a fine son. He gave such a good testimony last Wednesday night at prayer meeting."

"You mean my son was at the prayer meeting last Wednesday night?" the father asked. "Oh, how I wronged him. I whipped him because I thought he had lied to me." The father went home to the son, begged his forgiveness, was reconciled and a wonderful family relationship developed.

Then, to cap the illustration, Gothard cites I Peter 2:20: "For what credit is it if when you do wrong and are beaten for it you take it patiently? But if when you do right and suffer for it you take it patiently, you have God's approval . . . "

When children think they are treated unfairly by their parents, Gothard suggests three steps for them:

1. Try to understand the reason why the parents did what they did.
2. Learn to develop a creative alternative.
3. Develop confidence in God's ability to bring about a changed decision.

Gothard then applies these three steps to the illustration of the young girl whose parents were opposed to her marriage even though she was convinced it was God's will. Gothard says their basic intention was not to restrict her happiness but rather to help her achieve lasting happiness. They intended to pass on to her the insights and lessons which they had learned, perhaps the hard way. They intended for her to avoid a lot of future complications which they knew they themselves would be involved in if she made the wrong choice in marriage. They intended to derive pleasure and joy from their daughter's marriage and looked forward to the possibility of grandchildren.

The creative alternatives that Gothard suggests for the young girl were these: Discuss with her parents the qualities she should look for in a husband. Give her parents ample opportunity to become acquainted with the boyfriend before there was any discussion of marriage. Ask her parents to point out areas where both she and her boyfriend could improve. Request that her parents set up guidelines to help her discern whether she has met the right life partner. Be willing to show deference to her parents on the timing of the engagement.

And, sure enough, God did change the decision of the parents. When the girl followed the alternatives listed above, her parents recommended a three-year wait to allow the fellow to finish his education and to get financially prepared for marriage. They felt that if he wasn't the right one, the interest would diminish. During this time, however, both developed inward qualities which increased the respect of her parents for the boy and resulted in the parents' full approval of the marriage. On their wedding day, her father said with tears in his eyes, "This is the happiest day in my life!"

This matter of being under authority is so important in Gothard's approach that his syllabus contains a series of questions and answers, such as "How old do I have to be before I'm out from under authority?" His answer is that we never outgrow the need to be under authority; we are commanded to be under authority at all times.

When does the parental "chain of command" end? It ends only when the parents delegate that authority to someone else—as in marriage or the ministry.

What if I'm an adult and still single? Gothard suggests that if by that time you have not earned a position of being in a "chain of counsel," there must be some serious deficiency in your attitude or understanding. Furthermore, whatever your age, you are always to be responsive to your parent's counsel. To prove this, Gothard cites Proverbs 23:22: "Hearken unto thy father that begat thee, and despise not thy mother when she is old."

Under whose authority am I if my parents are divorced? The parent who is legally responsible for you becomes your direct chain of command. The separated parent may be a part of your chain of counsel. If the parent with whom you are living remarries, they automatically delegate part of their authority to your step-parent.

What if I'm still single and living in an apartment?

Gothard's reply: "First, be very sure that God has led you to move away from your parents, and that they were fully in harmony with the move. When God designed the family structure, He purposed that each one in the family meet basic needs for the others—especially social needs. When a single person leaves his family, he exposes himself to many unnecessary temptations to wrongly fulfill these social needs. If your parents are in full harmony with your move to another location, it is important to maintain good lines of communication with them in order to receive counsel from them.

What if I'm a widow or divorced? Your direct line of authority would be to God, Gothard says. However, it would be very essential to build around your life as many godly counselors as you can, especially parents and parents-in-law. God takes special care of the widow. He is their protector: "A father of the fatherless, and a judge of the widows, is God in his holy habitation" *Psalm 68:5*. If you are divorced and your former husband is not remarried, take whatever steps you can to be reunited. By so doing, you will be able to get back under his "umbrella of protection" and allow God to work through the marriage to achieve Christ's character.

What if I married the wrong person? Says Gothard: Your marriage may not have been one that God would have arranged; however, since He has established the authority of the marriage relationship, He will use whatever marriage you enter into to perfect His character in you. When your ways please the Lord, He will even make your enemies to be at peace with you *(Proverbs 16:7)*. This will happen to an even greater degree with your life partner.

The Husband-Wife Relationship

Attitudes in the world are such today that while many people will accept more or less readily that parents ought to have authority over the children, and perhaps even grant that there has been too much permissiveness, the current emphasis on women's liberation makes it a little more difficult to accept the authority relationship of the husband over the wife too. But Gothard is deadly serious in insisting that that is precisely what is proclaimed in the Bible.

Obviously, the husband has no right to be a tyrant, but if he is a tyrant nonetheless, then God must have a purpose for it, and it may well be through the wife that this purpose is carried out. Again, she has to develop creative alternatives and then maintain confidence in God's ability to bring about a change in the husband. And from his inexhaustible resource of stories, Gothard can find many illustrations that prove that this indeed can be done, and often is done.

While this may be the one aspect that many wives take with tongue in cheek, there are also many who are earnestly convinced that this is God's way, and they are not only willing to submit to it, but are very happy with it—women's liberation notwithstanding. In fact, they *feel* just as much liberated as the wife who insists on equality with her husband.

I remember attending a meeting once, sponsored by Campus Crusade, which has much the same approach on this matter as does Gothard. There were about 500 at the meeting and about 50 of them were women. The language of all of the speakers was totally male oriented: "God chooses *men* to do his work . . . . Now, when you pastors get home, choose a strong core group of *men* . . . . And to the question whether they might be women, the definite answer was No."

Going up the elevator one day with several of the women at the conference, I said, "The part of the country I come from has quite a strong movement of women's liberation. I was just wondering, how do you react to all this male language around here and the emphasis that all of this must be done by men?"

Almost in unison, all three women said, "Oh, we're very happy that way. We think it is the function of the woman to be submissive. That's one of the problems in the world today, women are too selfish and independent."

Problems with the Authoritarian View

The basic disagreement that I have with Gothard concerning the chain of command comes down to our differing methods of Biblical interpretation. I believe that scripture ought to be read with an eye to the particular culture that was the immediate audience. Taking that into account, we can then look for what overall guidelines transcend cultural limitations and apply at all times.

The culture of the times was an extremely authoritarian culture. Women and slaves were at the bottom of the ladder. It's not surprising that this culture was reflected in the stories and illustrations given in the Bible. If I understand Gothard correctly, when God chose the Hebrews as the people through whom to reveal His plan of salvation, He also approved their authoritarian culture as the most desirable and the only authentic one, totally in keeping with His own will.

I would argue that God chose them out of grace, not because of the good that was in them, but because of what He could make of them. His choice of them did not approve their cultural patterns, nor all of their family customs. And yet God doesn't seem to rail at them for some of the marriage patterns, for instance, which are a long way from Christian standards of today. Even the story of David and Bathsheba shows the wrath of God kindled not as much against David's roving eye and passion for a beautiful woman taking a bath as for the fact that he stole Uriah's property (his wife) and then had him killed.

I cite this simply to point out that we will probably never convince each other by quoting scripture. Gothard is dealing with an important issue that needs to be taken seriously, but I feel that he has become preoccupied with an authoritarian pattern of human relationships that is not balanced sufficiently with love as a model.

Not only does our interpretation of scripture hinder our agreement, but we also cannot convince each other by use of success stories to strengthen our case. Gothard will have a tendency to tell all those stories that support his approach—stories literally by the hundreds of relationships between husbands and wives and parents and children that were completely out of whack until they agreed to follow the chain of command, and then everything worked out fine.

I could point to just as many stories of lives that were utterly miserable under a strict authoritarian tyranny. I'm not at all suggesting that Gothard approves of this tyranny. He regrets it just as much as I do. The difference is, he insists there is only one way of dealing with it and that is to submit to it and God will take care of the situation, and he can point to instances where that has happened. Furthermore, when I point to instances where this not only has not worked but has led to misery, he will always have the advantage of being able to say, "But they didn't really try it long enough or sincerely enough."

A Guilt-Inducing System

Earlier on this very day that I am writing these words, I went to a prayer group attended by about 30 people. A number of them described their family situations and asked for prayer support. Three of them said that their children were rebelling against them. Then one of the women prayed, "Oh God, help particularly us women so that we do not rebel against our husbands, because by our rebelling we are teaching our children to rebel." I couldn't help but think of the amount of guilt that women were having laid on them, that they were in fact the cause of their children's rebellion against them.

One person who attended a seminar described his reaction this way:

"There seemed to be a lack of teaching on God's acceptance, or on the spontaneous growth that comes from a loving, accepting relationship. Instead, consequences of principle violations are given as the sole motivation for growth. Personal moral failure is the prime motive for living a godly life. The system cannot stand unless the students are convinced that all pathology can be traced to moral guilt."

I talked to a pastor of a congregation that regularly sends about 100 members to the Institute seminars every time Gothard comes to town. I asked him what the effect was on these people. His reply was this:

"Those who are basically healthy to begin with are helped. They find many useful things to improve their already good situation. They do not accept everything Gothard says, however. They take a look, and reject what they think is not good and have no guilt feelings about it at all. They are strong members of our congregation."

"But those who are already rather rigid and legalistic to begin with," he said, "simply have their legalism and rigidity re-enforced. We've had a number of them leave our congregation because they just don't think we are strict enough. A neighboring pastor from a very evangelical church tells me the same thing."

Two other illustrations: A woman who thinks highly of the seminars and who was somewhat critical of my article, "The Pros and Cons of Bill Gothard," said to me: "I used to have a very good relationship with my boss. He was kind. I thought we worked together well. We respected each other. We cooperated and I worked hard. Then he went to a Institute in Basic Youth Conflicts seminar, and ever since then he has been much harder to work for. He now has the idea of authority, and we no longer have the spirit at work we used to have."

A friend told me, "I have a sister and brother-in-law, who have just the greatest family. They have two children, both below 10. There is an excellent relationship between the parents and the children. The kids get along well with each other and with their parents. It's just the kind of ideal family I'd like to have. Then the father went to the Institute in Basic Youth Conflicts, and now everything is changed. He's an authoritarian tyrant. The kids are getting nervous. Something happened."

It seems that Gothard fails to adequately present the need for relationships with children, positing instead the proper role and proper discipline that is necessary to get a desired response from the children. The preoccupation is with control, predictability, the proper behavior instead of the need for nurturing relationships in which learned behavior and attitudes come from *models, not coercive manipulation.*

I am by no means saying this happens to everyone who goes to a seminar. There are literally hundreds of thousands who find them most helpful. Nor am I saying that the actions of the father and boss described above should have been the logical outgrowth of their having attended a seminar. I am not saying that people should not go to seminars for fear that they will have the kinds of experiences described above. I am saying, however, that they should go with open minds, to accept all the good they find, but also to beware of some of the dangers.

Chapter 7

SPIRIT, SOUL, AND BODY

A Great Mystery

The day a child is taught his first evening prayer—
if it is the prayer most children learn—he is introduced to
one of the great mysteries of the ages.

"Now I lay me down to sleep,
I pray the Lord my soul to keep;
If I should die before I wake,
I pray the Lord my soul to take."

And if he should ask his mother, "Mommy, what's a
soul?" she would be hard put to give an answer, for the mere
fact that she is much older does not mean that the mystery
has been removed.

If the child comes from a Christian home, words such
as soul and spirit become a natural part of his vocabulary.
His grandmother dies, and he is told, "Her body is dead,
but her soul went to live with Jesus."

The words of David, the Psalmist, "I am fearfully and
wonderfully made," apply to us all. We know there is something more to the human being than the body. There is a
difference between the corpse lying in a casket and the per-

son standing by, talking. The bodies may essentially be the same, but the one is alive and the other is not.

This is another one of those instances where we are confronted with a mysterious reality that partakes of the divine, and all we have with which to describe it is a human language. No wonder we have difficulty. No wonder either that because of the complexity of the mystery different people will describe the mystery in different ways, each according to his or her own understanding as he or she feels enlightened by the scriptures.

Three Ways of Viewing Spirit, Soul, and Body

There are essentially three approaches in explaining this complex phenomenon: unity, dichotomy, and trichotomy. They are not automatically mutually exclusive. In fact, most people will hold some aspect of all three of these approaches, but then zero in on one of them as the overarching explanation.

The *unity* approach emphasizes the wholeness of the personality, recognizing of course that there is a body that can be seen, but also recognizing that there are other elements which cannot be seen but without which there cannot be life. Although they would locate the mind in the brain, there is still a difference between brain and mind. Nevertheless, they constantly emphasize the *whole person* rather than the various elements that compose the person.

Dichotomy usually speaks of body and soul. Many Christians hold this view. They take the Genesis account very seriously. God formed Adam out of the dust of the ground and then breathed in his nostrils the breath of life, and man became a living *soul* (*Genesis 2:7*). These Christians usually believe that at death the soul leaves the body, goes to live with God, and then on resurrection day is reunited with the body.

Trichotomy speaks of body, soul and spirit.

Gothard is essentially a trichotomist, and since his understanding of body, soul, and spirit pervades his whole thinking and his whole theology, an entire chapter will be devoted to this subject. He says that he uses this tripartite division of the human personality only as a teaching device to help us understand the mystery of the complex make-up of the human being and does not believe that the several aptitudes of body, soul, or spirit are actually localized somewhere. He also believes in a unity of the personality, and his emphasis constantly is on the fact that these three elements—body, soul, and spirit—must be properly *balanced* for a healthy personality.

He devotes nine pages in the syllabus to charts, diagrams, and explanations of the relationship of body, soul, and spirit. In every one of them, spirit is at the top, because it is always the most important.

The first diagram is a simple listing of the characteristics of each. It's useful here to also use the Greek words, as Gothard himself does, because sometimes there are two Greek words that are translated the same in English, and the choice of the translation that is used will have an effect on the interpretation.

The Greek word for spirit is *pneuma*, and the faculties assigned to the spirit are comprehension, conscience, insight, sensitivity, creativity, and motivation.

The Greek word for soul is *psuche*, and there are no faculties assigned to the soul in this diagram, but in the following diagram this is enlarged upon.

The Greek word for body is *soma*. (There is also another Greek word for body, *sarx*, and that is the word referred to in the following diagram.) But in this diagram, the faculties assigned to the *soma*, the body, are seeing, hearing, feeling, tasting, and smelling.

The second diagram chart is entitled, "The Basic Structure of Our Inner Personality," and contains this introductory sentence: "An understanding of the faculties of the soul is essential to understanding the conflicts which we experience and also the potential development of our inner being."

This chart now enlarges upon the faculties of the *psuche*. They are the mind, the faculty of knowing; the affections, the faculty of experiencing various emotions; and the will, the faculty of choosing, purposing, and deliberately designing.

Struggle Between Flesh and Spirit

But now Gothard does an interesting thing. Instead of listing the bottom part of this diagram as body, using the Greek word *soma* he uses the term "lower nature" *(sarx)*, and then has this comment:

"*Sarx:* The weaker element in our human nature (one New Testament use of the word, 'flesh'). This segment of the diagram now does *not* represent the body but the unregenerate condition of a person whose spirit has not yet been reborn (*Romans 7:5; 8:8* and 9). It represents the source of wrong impulses (*II Peter 2:18; I John 2:16*). After the spirit is reborn, the *sarx* represents the carnal or sensual side of a Christian (*Galatians 3:3; 6:8*)."

The third diagram is headed, "The Basic Conflict of Our Inner Personality." Here Gothard says, "Two forces within us become quite obvious as we attempt to fulfill that which we know to be right. One force seeks to draw our attention to the wrong impulses, the other seeks to draw our attention to the right impulses. The resulting struggle is well described in the words of Romans 7:15-25."

These verses in Romans are the ones where Paul describes his own agonizing behavior. The good things he wants to do, he somehow doesn't seem to do; but the evil he wants to avoid, he ends up doing. There is no doubt about it, virtually all Christians experience this kind of inner struggle or basic conflict.

This chart shows two magnets, one at the top identified as conscience and spirit; one at the bottom, identified as lower nature. Between these two are the faculties of the soul *(psuche),* mind, emotions, and will, in conflict, being pulled toward both magnets.

The next five charts then show that when the spirit (always at the top) is reborn, its power will gradually flow down to influence the mind, the emotions, and the will.

There is a very clear pattern of progression. "At our personal invitation," says Gothard, "the Spirit of Christ enters our spirit and by this we establish a living relationship with God. Without the Spirit of Christ, we have no relationship with God." There are now several initial evidences of God's Spirit in our life. Gothard lists three:

1. *A spiritual hunger for God's Word.* Now that our spirit has been made alive, it needs to be fed. The nourishment of the spirit is the Word of God *(I Peter 2:2).* Without a consistent intake of the Word, we will never discover successful living.

2. *A new sensitivity to right and wrong.* When the Spirit of God unites with our spirit, our conscience is strengthened. However, our mind, emotions and will continue to manifest conflicting thoughts, emotions and desires. The result is a hidden conflict in our inner personality until the Word of God is able to transform our mind, emotions, and will.

3. *A desire for a transformed life.* The image of Christ which our spirit can now more fully comprehend makes us dissatisfied with our former life and produces a desire to become more and more like Jesus Christ *(Romans 8:29* and *12:2).*

Once the Spirit of God has entered our spirit and given us a rebirth, our new life must now be nurtured. The essentials of that nourishment are the scriptures and prayer. Gothard explains how this can be done in seven steps: 1. Memorize whole thoughts and ideas from scripture. 2. Expand the meaning of key words. 3. Saturate your mind with scripture. 4. Turn memorized scripture into personal prayer. 5. Turn irritations, disappointments, heartaches into spiritual motivation. 6. Discover what God wants to accomplish.

7. Analyze the frustrations caused by spiritual deficiency.

Gothard has much scripture to fall back on. We have already referred to St. Paul's own struggle and conflict within himself. Many Christians have experienced similar struggles and have found that "living in the Word," as Gothard recommends, gives them the strength to overcome temptations and lead a satisfying life.

The section of the seminar manual containing all these various charts is called "Successful Living." Gothard's purpose seems to be twofold:

1. to show how the different parts of the total person function.
2. to show how the flesh and spirit struggle against each other.

He has made it clear that in the second section he is not referring to the body (*soma*) as the culprit in our struggle for success, but has introduced flesh (*sarx*) as the antagonist to spirit.

The Place of the Physical

Even though Gothard is careful to make the above distinction there is an element in his lectures that suggests the body itself is this lower nature that must be constantly subjugated. One of the ways in which Gothard's strong feeling comes out in this area is his absolute stand against rock music. Bill first began questioning the propriety of rock music when many of his alumni came to him and said, "Bill, we have a problem. We've tried everything you told us. We've gotten all bitterness out of our lives. We find it easy to forgive. We love the scriptures. But something just isn't right."

Bill was disturbed by this, and so when he began questioning them he found that one thing they all had in common was that they listened to rock music. To help them he developed a grid of basic principles of music evaluation.

The left column of the grid lists the three basic parts of the human personality—the spirit at the top, the soul in the middle, and the body at the bottom. The next column lists the basic parts of music. Melody ranks highest. It's in line with spirit. It's the more creative. It raises the spirit to God. Supporting this, Gothard quotes Ephesians 5:18-19: "And be not drunk with wine wherein is excess; but be filled with the Spirit; speaking to yourselves in psalms and hymns and spiritual songs, singing and making *melody* in your heart to the Lord."

Harmony is the basic part of music that is the counterpart of the soul. It includes the arrangements of chords in support of the melody. Rhythm is the basic part of music that belongs to the body.

These three must all be in balance. If there is too much melody and not enough harmony or rhythm, the basic effect will be tension, unfulfillment, frustration and the result may be depression and despair.

If there is too much harmony without a strong melody line the result is confusion and rebellion, too much showmanship and gushy sentimentalism. Rhythm ranks at the very bottom, along with the body. It calls forth the sensual nature. It can be proved, said Gothard, that a loud repetition of a rhythmical beat is appealing to the lower nature, which is expressed in bodily actions. And he asserts, "Those who don't believe this are either naive or dishonest."

A strong statement like that is pretty hard to disprove, when the one who has just espoused it has already called the intelligence and integrity of anyone who disagrees with him or his researchers into question. This kind of approach is of course seldom limited to one side of an argument. One of the quickest ways to dispose of an argument contrary to your own is simply to say that the other side is either stupid or dishonest. It would do very little good to line up other authorities, equally intelligent and equally committed to Christ, who might hold different views. There's not much you can do when you reach that kind of impasse. And all the more pity, because both sides probably have some valuable insights from which the other, as well as all of us, could benefit.

"This matter of the music we listen to is more important than we realize," Gothard says. "If you are a fan of rock music, you cannot have victory in your moral life until you change your music. It is sensual, and you can't combine the sensual with the spiritual."

Gothard applies a similar spirit-soul-body division to the whole subject of sexuality. Although he frequently affirms that sex is a gift of God, reserved for use only within the marriage, he says the emphasis on it must be balanced.

It's not sex, he says, because it does not exist in and of itself, but must be taught within a framework of values, and the public school is not the place to inculcate values. And it's not education, he says, because everybody knows that the best form of education is learning by doing, and therefore if young people are taught the facts of the sex act they will want to experiment and do it.

He is very much opposed to the kind of counseling that would help people improve their sex life by trying to discover what the difficulty might be. He warns all counselors not to probe into these intimacies. There are two reasons for this, he says. In the first place, it's against the Bible. Ephesians 5:12 says—after having just referred to the evils of immorality and impurity—that "it is a shame even to *speak* of the things that they do in secret." The other reason is that if counselors get too detailed in discussing these problems, they themselves may get tempted to immorality.

There are, of course, many who would agree completely with Gothard, because they too are fed up with our sex-crazed age. And at times the best way to deal with an illness is the major surgery of eradication instead of the gentle use of medication to bring a situation to health. Precisely because sex is flaunted at us from all sides and we see the morass it has caused in our national and personal lives, many people find it easy to agree with Gothard entirely.

Another one of the implications of this tendency of equating the physical world with the lower nature is that large sections of learning are considered inappropriate for Christians.

Church leaders have said, "We are sorry to see Gothard leave the impression that Christian young people should avoid the social sciences and humanities. This reflects his experience in the graduate program of psychology of Northwestern University, where he made the discovery that either he had to drop out or seriously jeopardize his faith."

They also disagree with Gothard's sub-Christian view of vocation that "your employment is only the means of your support." "Apparently," say the church leaders, "for Gothard, work has no intrinsic value except as it contributes to 'developing a life message.' This undercuts the New Testament view of vocational calling which teaches that we are to do all we do with all our might to the glory of God. More than that, it slights the creation mandate with its focus on such work as agriculture, industry, medicine, etc. Genesis 1:28 gives meaning and purpose to man's work that is quite apart from any specifically spiritual or pietistic byproducts."

The alternative to this is illustrated by the answer a man gave when someone asked him, "What's your occupation?"

He answered, "I'm a Christian."

"No, that's not what I mean," the questioner said, "I mean, what do you do?"

Again the man replied, "I'm a Christian, but I work in the meat packing plant to get money to pay expenses."

In reality, however, there is a much closer relation between the daily occupation of a person and his Christian faith than merely a paycheck that enables him or her to support the church.

Part of the will of God is to feed hungry people.

Who does God use to feed hungry people? He uses farmers to grow grain. He uses manufacturers who make tractors that the farmers can use to grow grain. He uses food processors to process the grain, commercial industries to transport and market the grain, etc. All of these industries are pleasing in God's sight and they do not suddenly receive a higher value because income earned from these occupations is used to support the church and missionaries.

An Evaluation

Gothard's subtle deprecation of the physical is unwarranted, especially in light of the incarnation and creation itself. The doctrine of the incarnation is more than simply the fact that Jesus was truly born as a man and became fully human. But in the incarnation, God once again tied Himself to the earthly creation that He had once made and of which He said over and over again that *it is good.*

(Unfortunately the view of the physical as evil comes down to us from Platonic Greek thought through some of the early church fathers, but the position cannot be supported from scripture.)

Regarding Gothard's views on rock music and sex, I find that he is again guilty of deciding what he would like scripture to say and then violating a text to prove his point.

In the case of music, Gothard is so caught up with his preconceptions and his outlines that he comes to some very strange conclusions. He begins by dividing a piece of music into three parts (to correspond to his three parts of man): melody, harmony, rhythm. This division itself is inaccurate since it implies that rhythm is a third component of music in the same category as melody and harmony. In actuality, harmony and melody in a song both conform to a particular rhythm.

Next, Gothard appeals to scripture to show that melody ranks the highest (in line with spirit on the chart) because it raises the spirit to God. Ephesians 5:18-19 says "And be not drunk with wine wherein is excess; but be filled with the Spirit; speaking to yourselves in psalms and hymns and spiritual songs, singing and making *melody* in your heart to the Lord."

"To make melody" is the translation of the Greek word *ado* which comes from Old Testament usage and means "to sing (to the accompaniment of a harp)." Gothard's whole point is thus based on an equivocation, where he assumed that the use of the word melody meant the main line of a song, when it didn't mean that at all. This is obviously a minor point, but it should make the reader very suspicious of careless prooftexting.

In Gothard's views on music he also violated the empirical evidence by saying that "the basic effect" of too much melody "will be tension, unfulfillment, frustration and the result may be depression and despair." I'm not sure what is meant by all this. "Too much melody" I suppose means melody with no harmony, but Gothard would be hard pressed to show how all these traumas could come upon a group of people singing in unison.

Gothard's whole case against rock music is very questionable. I personally don't care for rock music, but I don't know enough about the matter to decide for other people.

Regarding his view against counseling people to improve their sex life, I again find a violation of the text used to substantiate his position. Ephesians 5:11,12 says for Christians to "have no fellowship with the unfruitful works of darkness, but rather reprove them. For it is a shame even to speak of those things which are done of them in secret."

Gothard points out that this follows a passage on immorality, but he fails to note that there are at least six more "works of darkness" listed so that the passage is by no means directed toward discussing sexual matters. Rather it appears that Christians are being admonished not to discuss the sins of others.

Indeed, if Gothard insists on his own interpretation I'm afraid he will find the passage proving too much, because if the "things done in secret" of verse 12 are legitimate sexual acts within marriage, then we are not told in verse 11 to "reprove them." More likely the passage refers to gossiping about evildoers.

Finally, I see counseling those with sexual problems to be a positive approach. Sex is a good thing, and the burden of proof is on Gothard to show why anything of value should not be preserved, repaired or improved upon.

Chapter 8

DATING-MARRIAGE-FAMILY

A Pattern for Dating

"This is the time you have been waiting for all week," Bill Gothard announces as the seminar goes into its final stretch on Saturday afternoon. The subject for discussion is that universal favorite among all teen-agers: Dating and Marriage.

"Next to our salvation there is no more important item in life than marriage," says Gothard. The sentence hardly needs underlining. Given a few minutes of time virtually anyone can come up with half dozen or more illustrations of people whose lives have become absolutely miserable because of a bad marriage. Gothard is convinced that most of the broken marriages come about because of unhealthy dating practices. Successful marriages have their beginning in a healthy dating pattern.

"I'm firmly convinced that God never intended girls to turn down dates," says Gothard. But before the delighted girls can let their grins develop to full smiles,

Gothard completes the sentence, "It's God's plan that the girl's *father* should turn down the dates."

One of the popular stereotypes by which the Gothard seminars have become known, and dismissed by those who would laugh at them as being so mid-Victorian and Puritan that nobody could take them seriously is that he actually tells a girl that when a boy asks her for a date, she should tell him to ask her father. The first tendency of many modern day "with-it" people is to hoot at the idea.

One sixteen year old girl who was rather intrigued by the idea and really bought it, was asked, "How many of the teenagers in your group were willing to go along with Gothard on that idea?" Her reply: "Out of approximately 30 young people in our group, I would say that about half of them bought it." She was the second daughter in her family, and she went on to say, "My sister's boyfriends never did this, but I'm going to follow that practice myself. Dad may die of a heart attack, but that's just a chance I'll have to take."

Thus Gothard launches a discussion that has caused his seminars often to be stereotyped as Victorian and Puritan. He makes a good theoretical case, however, for the fact that if a boy thinks enough of a girl that he is willing to ask her father if he can date her, he is paying the girl a compliment. He defends his position in the following way:

1. What a fellow has to work for he appreciates more.

2. Having to ask the father decreases the temptation to mistreat the girl. Boys find it easier to mistreat a girl if they know she is not under someone's authority or guardianship.

3. A girl insisting that the boy ask her father is thereby proving that her father loves her.

4. In this way the girl is letting another man evaluate the motives of a man. Girls are no match for evaluating motives of a man, Gothard says.

5. This procedure also puts the boy under proper authority.

While the precise follow-through of this method may not be practiced, think about your own situation—either your own dates or the dates of your children. Isn't it true that if you had any kind of healthy relationship with your parents or your children, there was some kind of mutual understanding that parents had to approve the boy you or your daughter dated? What Gothard is calling for is that this kind of practice be intensified and made more explicit.

To illustrate that it is not so outlandishly old-fashioned for a girl to insist that a boy ask her father for permission to date her, Gothard tells the delightful story of the girl who was at college, a thousand miles away from home. When the first boy asked her for a date, she said, "My father and I have a very good relationship and we have an understanding that anyone who asks me for a date must ask him first."

"Sure, be glad to," the boy answered, "but how do I ask him when he's a thousand miles away?"

"Well, there is the telephone, you know."

The boy was taken aback a bit, but he did call, and he found her father so delightful that they developed an immediate friendship. Of course, it developed into the ideal marriage. The verbal and head-shaking assent observed in the seminar audience points to a common desire for this kind of family relationship. Call it romantic, if you will. Gothard would call it Christian.

"God never intended it to be our responsibility to find a wife or a husband," says Gothard. "God finds the one best suited for us." He then tells the story of Isaac and Rebekah. Furthermore, parents are in a better position to help young people find the right life partner.

Marriage itself is the physical union of two people, but if that union is to have lasting qualities it must be preceded by activities in the life of the spirit and the soul. Dating is not to be a casual thing. While it is true that when you date someone you are not thereby announcing that you are going to marry that person, Gothard says that when you date someone you are thereby "putting your stamp of approval on marriage." It is someone that you think you *could* marry. The purpose of dating is to discover if there is indeed a oneness of spirit that holds possibility of growth.

Engagement is the time for more planning, to build for a oneness of mind and will and emotion. This is also a time for the two families to get to know one another better. Gothard makes much of the point that the marriage of two people involves more than just those two people. It involves the entire family of both of them. If the first two steps, dating and engagement, have been carried out properly, the actual marriage, the physical union will be all the richer. And if there has not been proper preparation during these first two steps, the chances are that the last step, marriage, will not be as secure.

Gothard's View on Divorce

Gothard holds the strong view that there is absolutely no ground for divorce. He has a sublime faith that a right relationship with God can nurture a healthy marriage and stave off divorce for a shaky marriage.

Although Gothard has not changed his principles on divorce—he is very much against it at all times—he does say that his advanced seminars for pastors are giving more attention to how to work with the realities of those people who have been divorced and are remarried.

Gothard said, "When a couple comes to me to be married, I of course always ask them if they have been divorced. If they have then I literally hold my breath when I ask them the next question. I ask them if the former spouse is still single. If the answer is yes, then I breathe a sigh of relief, for I am convinced that God can bring them back together again, no matter how serious the rift was."

More attention is given to how to work with broken marriages for which reconciliation seems to be an absolute impossibility. He refuses, however, to say anything about these possibilities in the basic seminar. "After all," he says, "we must not hold anything except the ideal before these young people; otherwise they would too easily settle for less than the ideal."

What bothers me about this approach is the seeming implication that if good and bad alternatives are placed before young people they will have a tendency to gravitate toward the bad, and the way to avoid that is simply to keep them ignorant about the bad alternative. Aside from the impossibility of living in a world where people can be kept in the dark about very many things, ignorance is not one of the best ingredients in character building.

The Responsibility of Women

A major aspect that Gothard emphasizes in relation to divorce is that although divorce is always wrong, the burden for being involved in a divorce falls heavily on women. In his lectures he says that he gives his pastors' seminar a list of 22 consequences if a woman initiates divorce action. Although Gothard writes that "the man must be the spiritual leader," there is a great deal of responsibility placed on the wife.

"Don't put pressure on your husband if he wants to get a divorce," Gothard advises the wife. "Get your life in order with God and God will put pressure on the man. If you married a man who is divorced, it is important for you to call his former wife and ask her to forgive you. You wronged that first wife. You have a responsibility to the husband to see that he fulfills his responsibility to his first wife, particularly by supporting their children."

Another of Gothard's strong denouncements is against the working wife. Again, he has stories that illustrate the dangers involved. For instance, there is the pastor who told him that his wife had worked the first few years after they were married to put him through seminary, but years later they were divorced and he had to leave the parish.

Gothard very graphically illustrates the situation of a wife who works outside the home as a secretary. "In the first place," he says, "she is always nicely dressed when she goes to work. Her task really is to please her boss, so she naturally tries to be pleasant to him. And if she is a good secretary and her boss is eager to keep her he will try to be pleasant to her; so the relationship between a good boss and a good secretary is always a pleasant one."

"When she comes home, however," Gothard says, "she is faced with the housework. She'll undoubtedly change to some more grubby clothes. Furthermore she may well be tired from her day's work at the office and tend to be irritable. The result is that whereas her boss will usually see her at her best, her husband will frequently see her at her worst."

The same holds true for the boss, Gothard says. When he goes home to his wife, he may not be at his best either. What could be more normal, therefore, than for the boss and secretary, who more often see each other at their best instead of at their worst, to develop an affection for each other and have an affair that will break up the two homes.

This, of course, is precisely what happens many times. What compounds the tragedy still more is that the new marriage is in equal danger of breaking up because the boss and secretary who have been seeing each other at their best will also see each other at their worst as husband and wife.

It is difficult to separate Gothard's view of the family from his chain of command which always places the husband over the wife. And in the area of family friction (for whatever reason) Gothard appears to treat the wife not only as subordinate but inferior.

He feels that a wife ought to tell her husband about her feelings of frustration and unhappiness, but that she makes a big mistake if she also tries to diagnose why she is unhappy or what to do about it. Although Gothard constantly emphasizes the fact that a couple should work through their problems together, what subtly always seems to come through is that it is the inferior insight of the wife matched with the superior insight of the husband that makes for proper understanding. When wives make the jump from describing symptoms to also offering a diagnosis and recommending treatment, trouble begins, Gothard says.

The logic of this seems to me to break down, however, when he gives his next illustration. "Many husbands have told me," Gothard says, "that they were completely unaware that their wives were unhappy. One told me that one night he was sitting reading the paper and his wife came in all dressed up and said, 'Well, I'm leaving.' He said, 'Fine, I'll see you when you get home.' 'No, you don't understand,' the wife said, 'I'm leaving home; I'm leaving for good.'" This was the first time that the husband had an idea that there was anything wrong in their relationship.

And yet Gothard implies that this husband who was so totally insensitive to the needs of his wife should now all at once become a reservoir of great insight when it comes to diagnosing the situation and recommending treatment.

Gothard does, however, offer some very practical suggestions to husbands for maintaining a happy family. Develop good manners, he says. Men often don't know how much good manners mean to a wife. Praise her for things she has done well. Write little notes to her. Tell her you love her, and when you say it, say it with your eyes also. Call every night when you're away from home.

The Model Wife

Quoting from the Bible as he does for all of his principles of family relationships, Gothard finds his most complete description of the dutiful and virtuous wife in the 31st chapter of Proverbs:

"Who can find a virtuous woman? for her price is far above rubies.... She seeketh wool, and flax, and worketh willingly with her hands.... She riseth also while it is yet night, and giveth meat to her household, and a portion to her maidens.... She layeth her hands to the spindle, and her hands hold the distaff. She stretcheth out her hand to the poor; yea, she reacheth forth her hands to the needy.... Her husband is known in the gates, when he sitteth among the elders of the land.... She openeth her mouth with wisdom; and in her tongue is the law of kindness. She looketh well to the ways of her household, and eateth not the bread of idleness."

Gothard would, of course, make allowances for the poetic language, for very few households spin their own wool anymore; but essentially this is his picture of the ideal wife taken straight from the Bible, and unabashedly he prescribes it as the ideal for a happy family life in the 20th century.

An Evaluation

In the area of dating Gothard is much more sophisticated than many people give him credit for. Just as with his chain of command emphasis he is really dealing with the much deeper subject of how we in our culture deal with the whole concept of authority, so in the area of dating he is calling attention to the fact that our culture has not developed an acceptable standard of how boys and girls meet each other in a way that can lead to marriage. Other cultures have marriages arranged by parents, and we usually are told only the bad sides of that system, not aware that there are also some positive aspects to it. At times past there was an accepted system of chaperones, also with some positives and some negatives. But our system has grown up without planning and parents have virtually lost control. When the rate of broken homes and the misery of parents and children who are victims of broken homes and broken marriages are considered, it is no wonder that many people feel that Gothard's alternative is worth a try.

Gothard is to be commended for his emphasis on the family and for the recognition that strong families are based on a Christian influence. One needs no lengthy study to prove that family life in our country is in trouble. Nor need one apologize for clinging so strongly to the idea of what family life could be, and not too readily giving in to tendencies that would make it easier for families to break up.

Concerning the breakdown of marriages, I cannot totally share Gothard's confidence that any marriage can be salvaged, but I do applaud that kind of high regard in which marriage is held. One of the problems of a more open concept of marriage is that couples can decide too quickly that it won't work, and at the slightest spat decide to call it off. It is often through disagreements and reconciliations that deeper understanding is built into marriage.

I too believe in a strong commitment to the life-long aspect of marriage as indeed God's ideal plan. The fact is, however, that we live in an imperfect world, and while Gothard may be able to give all kinds of illustrations where even the worst of marriage breakups have been reconciled, one could produce many counter-examples where greater harm has come from the avoidance of divorce. I also believe that there are acceptable grounds for divorce as well as grace for those who have gone through the experience, particularly for those who would eagerly desire to be reconciled but the other party simply isn't interested.

Concerning Gothard's analysis of the place of the

wife, I find it to be far too condescending. While there is ample evidence from scripture that the wife ought to submit to the authority of her husband, that in no way implies that she is inferior. Jesus Christ introduced a new age of freedom and equality before God, but with this equal standing we are also to recognize various gifts and talents. Christian husbands ought to encourage the areas in which their wives excel, for the edification of the wife, the marriage, and the Body of Christ. This attitude of equality between husband and wife still allows for there to be an order of authority that is Biblically sound. There is often a need for someone to take the lead, and the husband is merely the first among equals.

In accordance with Gothard's authoritarian view of the family, it is not surprising that he should focus on strict obedience.

As one critic has said, "Gothard seems to stress and direct most of his attention to the bottom of the chain, i.e., to the wife and not the husband; to the adolescent and not the parents; and to the employee and not the employer. In fact in the seminar there is nothing said about the correct attitude and behavior of those higher in the chain."

Actually one could just as easily focus on the duty of the husband to "love his wife as Christ loved the church." Instead of relying on the husband's position of authority to bring about an orderly, happy home, perhaps the husband ought to draw his family to obedience by the power of his love for them. Indeed, this is the model Christ offers: "We love Him because He first loved us," not because of His position of authority.

Regarding the "evils" of the working woman, Gothard again presented only one side of the picture. Indeed, there can be serious problems, but many examples can be given where a wife's working has been a good thing. To insist that a woman remain mainly in the home from her wedding day to her death is to rob the Christian community (and the community at large) of the benefits of her particular talents. Furthermore, it puts a great burden on a marriage to expect a husband, who is constantly growing, to find his wife still interesting over the years if she has done nothing (for pay or not) that keeps her growing. She may or may not need to leave the home to do this, but that is immaterial.

Finally, it is interesting that Gothard uses Proverbs 31 as illustrative of the model wife and yet insists that women should not work. Verses 16, 13 and 24 read as follows:

> "She considereth a field, and buyeth it: with the fruit of her hands she planteth a vineyard."
> "She seeketh wool, and flax, and worketh willingly with her hands."
> "She maketh fine linen, and selleth it; and delivereth girdles unto the merchant."

Yet, sprinkled among these verses are many which say she manages her home well while she continues to move about in the business world. Note also that her husband was apparently a leader in the town (v. 23), so one does not get the impression that she worked because of necessity.

This passage talks about a remarkable woman and it could well be that most women are not as capable. But it would be unwise to assume from the outset that this life-style is wrong at all times for all women, when scripture seems to indicate otherwise.

Chapter 9

12 STEPS TO MORAL PURITY

Many Useful Insights

As Gothard has frequently said, the best way to understand the principles of Christian living as he has outlined them in his Institute in Basic Youth Conflicts seminars is to attend one of the seminars. Better still, attend them several times, for they are so comprehensive that it is difficult to get them all in one experience. One could easily write a massive book based on his seminar syllabus, which is already rather massive in itself. The purpose of this chapter is to zero in on one particular lecture that I found particularly meaningful.

This chapter will be a very personal one. Also a very positive one. The actual title that Gothard gives to this part of one of his lectures is "12 Steps to Guard Sons and Daughters From Moral Impurity." No matter what kinds of problems people may have with what they might describe as Gothard's overly pious language, the simple fact of the matter is that moral purity is to be preferred over moral impurity. My wife and I have what we consider to be a Christian home. We were reared in Christian homes and we have tried to rear our two daughters in a Christian home. We feel that we have been successful and for this we are both extremely joyful as well as grateful to God.

I was very much impressed with the 12 steps that Gothard gave, and I concluded that though my wife and I may not have been consciously aware of these 12 steps and may have articulated some of them in different ways, we found them to be extremely well stated. In this chapter, therefore, I will essentially reflect on these 12 steps, relate them to our own family experience, and heartily commend them to all as a guide for good parent-child relationships.

Consecrate your child to God. Even for people who have lived a lifetime in the church and for whom "religious" language is as common as breathing, there come times when words become empty. You've said it so often and it's become so commonplace as to be almost sacrilegious. But "consecrate" has a simple dictionary meaning: "to devote to a purpose with deep solemnity or dedication." In this sense you *do* consecrate your children to God. Christian parents who recognize their children as gifts from God and consecrate them to God have an indescribable feeling of peace and joy and are convinced that life is meaningful because God has a place of prominence.

Teach the child to be alert to your spirit. This is a way of communication before the child is able to understand verbal language. Psychologists have discovered how very early in life—even within the first several hours—the child responds to acceptance or can be aware of rejection. "Be consistent," says Gothard. "Show the child happiness when he pleases you." If you yourself feel fully accepted by God and live in a state of grace, you can't help but show that to your child. He or she is sensitive and alert to your spirit long before he understands words. Taught early enough in life to be sensitive and alert to this spirit, children will develop an almost automatic and natural sensitivity also to what pleases you and what displeases you. If your life is a Spirit-filled life they will notice and will find it natural and easy to be comfortable with that kind of outlook on life.

Develop in the child the fear of God. Fear is a tricky word. It needs to be handled with care but it need not be avoided. Fear is a healthy emotion. We don't touch a hot stove because we are afraid of burning ourselves. We don't run across the street in front of a car because we are afraid of being hit. We obviously don't want to picture God as an ogre. He is a God of love, who cares for us and forgives. But neither is He an indulgent grandfather who grants our every wish no matter what it may do to us. God is a righteous and just God, who can be stern. To offend Him may result in dire consequences. Hence children should learn what those consequences are.

Some people might question one illustration that Gothard uses to emphasize this point. He describes a little boy about to steal some candy in a store, but then he sees a policeman watching him and he refrains from stealing. "Now put God in the place of that policeman," says Gothard. I don't particularly like an image of God as a policeman but somehow or other we do need to inculcate in our children a respect for a God of power who can and *will* destroy evil.

An emphasis that Gothard likes to develop is that God watches everything we do. He recommends a number of Bible passages and even suggests that we frame them so that they will be indelibly impressed upon our children, passages such as:

"Thou God seest me" *Genesis 16:13.*

"He that planted the ear, shall he not hear? he that formed the eye, shall he not see?" *Psalm 94:9.*

"Thou knowest my downsitting and mine uprising, thou understandest my thoughts afar off. Thou compassest my path and my lying down, and art acquainted with all my ways" *Psalm 139:2,3*.

"For the ways of man are before the eyes of the Lord, and he pondereth all his goings" *Proverbs 5:21*.

"The eyes of the Lord are in every place, beholding the evil and the good" *Proverbs 15:3*.

It's important to have a healthy balance, picturing God as a father, who is loving, but also as one who can be offended and for our own good will take action that may cause us pain.

Bring the child to personal salvation. This is just a natural path that any Christian parent would want to follow, but it doesn't happen automatically. This is what Christian nurture is all about—teaching the child to pray, taking him along to Sunday school and church, telling him about Jesus and His love, and demonstrating by word and example what acceptance of Jesus as personal saviour really means.

Give the child a sense of destiny. God has a special purpose for him. A child of God is a child of a King and has an inheritance fit for a king. God has a special and noble plan for everyone, and no one should write that off as insignificant. In other words, very simply, make your children feel important, because in the eyes of God they are important. Or, as the famous poster has it, "I know I'm important because God made me and God don't make no junk."

Guide the child to total dedication. Romans 12:1 is an important verse: "Present your bodies a living sacrifice, holy, acceptable unto God, which is your reasonable service." Three modern New Testament versions shed light on what this means.

"With eyes wide open to the mercies of God, I beg you, my brothers, as an act of intelligent worship, to give him your bodies, as a living sacrifice, consecrated to him and acceptable by him. Don't let the world around you squeeze you into its own mold, but let God remold your minds from within, so that you may prove in practice that the plan of God for you is good, meets all his demands and moves toward the goal of true maturity" *(Phillips)*.

"I implore you by God's mercy to offer your very selves to him: a living sacrifice, dedicated and fit for his acceptance, the worship offered by mind and heart. Adapt yourselves no longer to the pattern of this present world, but let your minds be remade and your whole nature thus transformed. Then you will be able to discern the will of God, and to know what is good, acceptable, and perfect" *(New English Bible)*.

"Offer yourselves as a living sacrifice to God, dedicated to his service and pleasing to him. This is the true worship that you should offer. Do not conform outwardly to the standards of this world, but let God transform you inwardly by a complete change of your mind. Then you will be able to know the will of God—what is good, and is pleasing to him and is perfect" *(Good News for Modern Man)*.

Train the child to discern character. God never intended that education should be taken totally out of the hands of parents. The home, under the guidance of parents, is the best place to build character and to help a child to understand what the ingredients of good character are. Gothard recommends that parents and children should systematically study the Bible together, not only to memorize verses and know Bible stories but to put together the various passages pertaining to particular characteristics. For instance, Gothard says, "There are 65 different attitudes described in the book of Proverbs alone. It would be a good project for parents and children to put together all the references pertaining to each attitude."

He tells the story of a mother overhearing a neighbor boy trying to get her son to do something that was wrong. Her son answered very calmly, "I don't think that would be wise." The parents had trained that child to discern character, to know almost by instinct what is right and wrong.

Encourage the child to stand alone. Perhaps nothing is as difficult for a child to learn as that sometimes he or she has to stand alone. The pressure of a peer group can be overpowering. The child should learn early in life that standing up for what is right sometimes means that you have to stand alone and suffer some rather unpleasant consequences. Gothard encourages parents to "Tell your son or daughter, 'I would rather have you get a zero in that assignment than to read a book that you know is pornographic.' "

Saturate your child's mind with scripture. A child should grow up with Bible stories as a part of everyday living.

Show your child the consequences of evil. "We hear and see much about what 'men of distinction' supposedly drink, but take your child to skid row and see what really happens to these 'men of distinction,' " says Gothard. One of the most devastating things in our classrooms, says Gothard, is that we teach all about perverted cultures but don't point out what some of the evil consequences of these perversions are.

Teach your child to witness and testify.

Support your child with fervent prayers.

How could anyone find fault with any of these 12 steps? Having them presented in this interesting and systematic way is a wholesome reminder and review of something that Christian parents undoubtedly already know.

What I mean to assert in this chapter is that many parts of the Institute in Basic Youth Conflicts seminars are extremely practical. It's somewhat like a writer who knows almost instinctively the rules of grammar—because he has been practicing them all along. But every now and then a review of the fundamentals is in order, and even the most mature writer will benefit.

This chapter in Gothard's seminar is an excellent review for child-rearing.

Chapter 10

ASK THE PERSON WHO'S BEEN THERE

Thousands of Satisfied Customers

There's a saying that the best way to find out about a product is to ask a satisfied customer. Or, another way of saying it, "The proof of the pudding is in the eating." It's no problem to find "satisfied customers" who paid their $35 or $45 for attending an Institute in Basic Youth Conflicts seminar and were well pleased with what they got. The problem for a writer is in paring down the large number willing to provide testimonials so as not to end up with a book too heavy to carry.

I'll always remember a former owner of five banks who told me of his experience. "I had moved to Minneapolis," he said, "and one day I got a long-distance call from a friend in Oregon. 'Bob,' he said, 'I've just been to the most important thing in my life. I went to one of Bill Gothard's Institute in Basic Youth Conflicts seminars. It'll cost you and your wife $55 to go, but I'm going to keep you on the telephone until you promise me that you'll go the next time he comes to Minneapolis.' " The banker and his family have since attended three seminars and are indeed satisfied customers.

Here are a few testimonials, the likes of which could be gathered by the bushel:

"I have attended two times and drove 165 miles one way each day and this fellow gave me a lot of help—in fact, more than anyone yet. I see the people who went along with me and what they learned has made a big difference in their homes."

"I was like a drowning man when I heard about the seminar. But today my wife and I are living together once more and loving one another. It's like a second honeymoon. Although I have a doctor's degree in theology from a leading evangelical seminary, I have never seen or heard the things brought out in this seminar."

An In-Depth Interview

Perhaps one in-depth interview with a "satisfied customer" will illustrate the kind of feelings many people have about the seminar. The name of this couple had been given to me by a pastor of a congregation which regularly sent more than 100 people to the seminar every time Gothard came to town. The pastor said this couple would give me a "fair" evaluation, one which was essentially positive about the seminar but "didn't buy everything Gothard had to say."

I made the appointment and they were eager to talk. They were a beautiful, Christian young couple. The husband, a dentist, was a Catholic; the wife a Lutheran. "Essentially positive," I soon discovered meant about 98% positive.

"It seemed to come along just at the right time," the husband said. "I wouldn't say our marriage was rocky, but with me being a Catholic and my wife being Lutheran, we naturally had our tensions. But the Institute in Basic Youth Conflicts seminar really did cement our marriage."

"I guess one of the big things to me," the husband said, "was the unique way of understanding God's will. We can now look at anything that happens that seems to be bad at the time and ask, 'I wonder what God is trying to teach us through this experience?' For instance, just the other day we had a calamity at the office, when a water pipe broke and my whole carpet was ruined. But I could come home and joke about it. God just wanted me to get a new carpet."

"How do you feel about the fact that you, as the wife, always end up in second place?" I asked.

"Well, it's not really true that I end up second place," she replied. "There simply is no such thing as two people being completely equal, whether they be two men or two women or a man and a woman. There come times when one person finally has to make a decision and the other person go along with it. I think that those who went for only one session may have found the chain of command kind of hard to take, but in the course of the week it is explained in such a way that it doesn't come across quite so harsh. In fact, the first night or so we were kind of floundering ourselves, but by Wednesday and Thursday nights, things just seemed to fall into place."

"Another thing that was most helpful," said the husband, "is that it erased all shades of gray. I'm convinced that God did not make gray. When it comes to moral issues, things are black or white. Whenever you're tempted to settle for shades of gray, you'll always have a tendency to come down on the side closer to wrong."

After the wife said, "We simply don't believe in situational ethics," I posed this problem: "Suppose you are upstairs taking a bath," I said to the wife. "And you are down in the living room reading the paper," I said to the husband, "and a man knocks at the door who appears quite suspicious to you. In fact, you rather quickly size him up as a rapist. And he asks you, 'Is your wife home?' what are you going to say?"

Without even pausing to think, the husband said, "I'd say no," but he and his wife quickly added, "but it would be wrong to do so."

Instead of shades of gray, he preferred to speak of degrees of white. "Some responsibilities are greater than others," he said. "I would have a greater responsibility to my family at that time than to tell the truth that would help a man to harm my wife."

The young husband and wife both spoke very strongly of the necessity of getting bitterness out of their lives and how Gothard showed them how to do this. They also gave numerous examples of others from their congregation who had similar experiences.

"How would you have felt if you were a divorced woman and had gone to a Gothard Institute?" I asked.

"Well, I must admit that would have been kind of rough," she said. "I have some very good friends who are divorced and they found that part of the seminar rather hard to take. But those who really tried to put into practice what Gothard told them found that it worked.

"For instance, one of my friends was involved in a very bitter divorce. Both of them have remarried. After she came back from the seminar she called her former husband and apologized, and although obviously they are staying married to their present spouses, the feeling of bitterness resulting from the first marriage has left entirely, and her former husband later became a Christian."

"It isn't, of course, that all that Gothard said was so totally new to us," the husband said. "We were essentially a Christian family and had many of the general feelings that Gothard expressed. But hearing them presented in the systematic way that Gothard has of presenting them just crystallized them for us."

"I was particularly impressed with Gothard's emphasis on yielding our rights to God," the wife said. "I used to demand my rights—my right to sleep for example—and then be bitter at my children for not allowing me that right. I now know I don't have that right. If I need sleep, God will see to it that I get it."

The husband and wife both agreed that some of Gothard's illustrations were too simplistic, that everything just seemed to work out right every time. They felt that Gothard was especially unrealistic in his strong stand against women working outside the home. This wife worked outside of the home part-time, apparently because of a need for an added sense of fulfillment.

But there was no mistake about it, this couple was thoroughly sold on the Institute in Basic Youth Conflicts, not only for what it had done for them personally, but also for the fellowship it had brought them with many other like-minded people.

Despite these very affirmative feelings expressed by many people who have attended a seminar, there are still those—myself included—who try to understand this amazing phenomenon of a movement that in many ways is so contrary to prevailing thought modes of the country but that nevertheless attracts so many people even though the cost in time and money is quite high.

Paul R. Keating, a marriage counselor in Haddonfield, N.J., and director of program planning and development at Hall-Mercer Community Mental Health Center in Philadelphia, writes in *Eternity* magazine:

"Nowhere, seemingly—and that's a sad commentary on the church—are young people, or anyone for that matter, being taught how to integrate Scriptural principles into a unified philosophy or psychology of life. Gothard, this generation's spokesman for the truths of the Keswicks, the camp meetings and the deeper life Bible conferences of earlier years, has done just that. What a relief for parents and teenagers to have some sane and agreed upon rules for dating patterns, respect for parents, exquisite maturity, Christian commitment. No wonder thousands at a time eagerly participate!"

In the same issue of *Eternity* two other Christian leaders write: "God has used the Institute in Basic Youth Conflicts to bring healing to countless lives. There's no doubt about that. Evangelicals need Bill Gothard's major thrusts. His insights on self-acceptance, forgiveness and one's relationship to parents are bold and forceful. What Gothard says about dying to ourselves—relinquishing our rights and finding them transformed by God's grace into privileges—is thoroughly Biblical and much-needed in this materialistic and individualistic day. And Gothard's emphasis on openness and confession should warm up some of our cold churches.

"Furthermore, his stress on putting our complete trust in the living God who acts in our lives and works out His will is absolutely necessary if faith is to be a live option in our secular world. In all this we have much to learn and Mr. Gothard has much to teach."

Reasons for the Seminar Appeal

Why then, in short, are the Gothard seminars so well attended?

1. *Certainty is more appealing than ambiguity.* In the pendulum swing of our society during the past few decades we experienced the social activist 60's, which found many of us floundering. Old standards were called into question. The stability of law and order was being questioned. It's obviously wrong to steal at the point of a gun. Although it's more sophisticated to cheat on your income tax, that's still stealing, but is it really as bad as stealing with a gun? It's also wrong to throw a brick through a window. But if that is finally the only way a group of people who have been victims of injustice can get attention and thus have their rights restored, was it altogether that wrong to throw a brick through a window?

Who is to say what is right and wrong and who has the right to determine for others what is right and wrong? Were we getting close to that darkest chapter in the history of Israel, described in the book of Judges as "every man did what was right in his own eyes?"

It would be much easier not to have to bother with all of these difficult questions of degrees of right and wrong and get back to some basics again where right is right and wrong is wrong. It is also easier to have someone who will decide for us. As the dentist said, "Gothard made plain to us that there are no shades of gray. God did not make any grays."

This feeling of certainty comes as a great relief to those who are tired of dealing with ambiguities. So there are those who are convinced that the reason Gothard has such a following is that people don't want to think; they want easy answers and Gothard gives them. They may not always be able to follow the instructions Gothard gives, but at least they will know right from wrong and know when to feel properly guilty. As the dentist said, if a man whom he suspected of being a rapist came to his door and asked if his wife was home, he would say, "No," but he would know that he had done something wrong in telling a lie.

2. *Beliefs formerly held with strong conviction, but under increasing question are vindicated again.* As the dentist's wife said, "I had a lot of things reaffirmed. Old values are not outdated. I don't feel quite so old-fashioned anymore."

Parents thought they were doing right by being rather strict with their children, but permissiveness seemed to be the prevailing mood of the times. And although parents had a gut-level feeling that they ought to be more strict, they were beginning to believe that maybe it was this strictness that had brought about the generation gap and had caused their children to reject them.

Gothard comes along and assures them, "No, you haven't been too strict with your children. If anything, you haven't been strict enough." They feel vindicated again. The fact is that children don't thrive in a completely permissive society. Parental discipline gives them more stability and a sense of being loved than does parental neglect, even though the neglect may have been intended as benign. There is an increasing recognition of the truth that a river without banks becomes a swamp. Barriers are as important to life as banks to a river.

Other "truths," or at least folklore that has long been held as self-evident, such as "the place of the woman is in the home" and "the man is the head of the house" are given new credence.

All of this is reinforcing and in keeping with the current mood of nostalgia that the good old days really had some values worth preserving even though they have undergone severe attack.

3. *The amazing power of God against seemingly insuperable odds still has an attraction for people.* Playing the role of "devil's advocate" in my interview with the dentist and his wife, I said, "Why is it that Gothard always comes down so hard on the wife? Isn't it possible that there is a husband who is just a plain louse? What kind of sense is it to encourage the wife to go to him and apologize for *her* actions? Isn't it possible that she is thereby just encouraging him in his irascibility and making it all the harder for God to get to him?"

"Not so," answered the dentist. "What could be more persuasive to a man who is a real louse than to have a long-suffering wife come to him and, of all things, apologize to *him* for the wrongs that *she* has done? Wouldn't that just tear at his heart?" And they could cite instances where precisely that had happened.

Is this perhaps what the Bible has in mind when it teaches that God's strength is made perfect through human weakness? When nothing else seems to work or to melt a hard heart but the unjust suffering, borne patiently, there is a sense of elation that the power of God indeed does work.

An earlier chapter in this book told the story of a high school youth who was unjustly whipped by his father who thought the boy had done something wrong and wouldn't listen to hear his side of the story. It was the listener who was enraged by the father's action, not the boy who took the whipping. The boy took his refuge in I Peter 2:20: "For what credit is it, if when you do wrong and are beaten for it you take it patiently: But if when you do right and suffer for it you take it patiently, you have God's approval."

The ways of human beings are simply not the ways of God. Haven't we been taught that from our youth? And aren't we still thrilled when we hear stories of the power of long-suffering, even as we are enraged by the injustice of it all?

Over and over again Gothard emphasizes the truth of Isaiah 55: "For my thoughts are not your thoughts, neither are your ways my ways, says the Lord. For as the heavens are higher than the earth, so are my ways higher than your ways and my thoughts than your thoughts."

Gothard counts on the fact—and his crowds seem to prove him right—that telling the ways of God still attracts people, perhaps all the more so when the ways of God seem so very contradictory to the ways approved by the majority of people. There is something in the pioneering American tradition that exults in the story of the underdog who wins against great odds.

Chapter 11

GOTHARD'S FUTURE PLANS

Future Plans Not Publicized

I would leave you under no illusion that Gothard has spelled out his long-range plans for me. Nor would I expect him to. He is rather closed-mouthed about publicly giving details of his future plans because of two fears, both of them justified. 1. People have a tendency to want quick success without doing the necessary hard work required for a disciplined program. I think Gothard is afraid that if too much of his plans are announced publicly, others will quickly pick up on aspects of it—not that he is afraid that they would "steal his thunder" but that they would develop a program that might have some of "the form of godliness but not the power thereof." 2. Gothard, as so many others, simply doesn't trust the press, not because he is afraid that they deliberately are dishonest and distort, but because they will mislead when they condense their material. He feels that for the story to be told properly it must be told in complete detail. That's why the Institute in Basic Youth Conflicts seminar itself is 32 hours long.

A *Basic Church Ministry*

He does, however, give some general descriptions of what he sees as basic challenges confronting his organization. One of these is what is known as a basic church ministry. In other words, the Institute in Basic Youth Conflicts is to be a tool placed at the disposal of an ever increasing number of local churches, demonstrating to the world a "new" approach to life, and helping the local churches to implement basic life principles into the daily experiences of their members.

For the local church to participate in a basic church ministry program as designed by the Institute in Basic Youth Conflicts, the senior pastor must first of all have attended a basic seminar. There must also be a sufficient number of alumni in the congregation who have attended a seminar so they can assist the pastor in implementing the objectives of the basic church ministry. The minimum of alumni required depends upon the size of the congregation and its distance from the nearest location of a basic seminar. For those churches located within 80 miles of a seminar or less than one-and-one-half hours driving time, 25% of the adult membership must have attended a seminar. A minimum of 30 is required. For churches further away than that or a membership of less than 200, a minimum of 15 is required.

"These requirements are based on much experienced counsel from many pastors," the promotional literature says. "They have urged us to maintain these requirements and have assured us that they are necessary in order for a church to gain the full benefit of the seminar ministry. In order to be fair to the thousands who have already been turned away from the Advance Seminar, it is essential for us to be consistent in these requirements. We are deeply appreciative for what we feel your attitudes and understanding will be in this regard."

A minister's manual, made available to senior pastors

only after they have qualified, has some of the following objectives:

Sermon guides, living testimonies, and personal conferences with men that will clarify the vision of what God wants to do through individuals, marriages, families, businesses, and the local church.

Sermon guides, workshops with wives, workshops with men, and living testimonies that will explain how the chain of command works in family, business, and church.

Determine that the church will follow God's principles in building successful marriages and dealing with broken marriages through sermon guides, an understanding of 22 consequences when the wife initiates divorce, how to deal with broken marriages, and workshops for fathers.

There is no doubt about it, this more formal program of providing a ministry to congregations will have a multiplying effect on the program that is now already reaching hundreds of thousands of people through the basic seminars.

Other Developments

Gothard announced to the ministers attending the basic seminar in Detroit that the Institute in Basic Youth Conflicts is making plans for expanding its program to other countries, with Australia probably being one of the first targets, because of the great interest that has been shown there. He also reported a great likelihood that the principles of character building inherent in the seminar are about to be used in many of the prisons in the country.

One of Gothard's dreams has long been to exert a heavy influence on the educational curricula of our country. He feels that there's where much of the damage is done that has resulted in a permissive society that has been destructive of character. He is convinced that all of education should be approached from the perspective of character building, and this can only be done if the principles of

God's Word are incorporated in the educational process. He is also convinced that absolutely every subject can be taught from that perspective.

Character Sketches

The first book is now off the press that is to make its mark in that field. The title is *Character Sketches*, with the descriptive line "from the pages of Scripture illustrated in the world of nature." It's a handsomely designed book printed by Rand McNally with a selling price of $35. It has been offered at some of the seminars at a special of $20. The Detroit seminar was one of the first for which it was available. Because of the high price the arrangements committee thought it might be able to sell 300 copies, but when the sale was announced, "It seemed that there were 3,000 requests for it," said one of the attendants. A van was sent to Chicago at two o'clock in the morning to bring more copies, and these too were all sold out before the seminar was over.

The idea behind this book also is based on the Bible. The back of the box in which the book is made available carries this scriptural rationale: "Now all these things happened unto them for ensamples; and they are written for our admonition, upon whom the ends of the world are come" *I Corinthians 10:11.* "But ask now the beasts, and they shall teach thee; and the fowls of the air, and they shall teach thee: Or speak to the earth, and it shall teach thee: and the fishes of the sea shall declare unto thee" *Job 12:7,8.*

The book is designed to "combine the teaching of character qualities with the teaching of academic facts; teach sons and daughters the principles of wisdom so that they will know how to integrate facts with daily living; and teach young men and women how to be mighty in Spirit so that they can discover the concepts of God and expose the misconceptions of man."

The 382-page, encyclopedia-size book contains seven parts and 28 sub-parts. Each of the sub-parts follows a similar format: a nature story; characteristics and physical features of the particular animal featured in the nature story; a scripture story; background about the person featured in the story; and a character sketch about the scripture personality.

For instance, the general subject of Part One is loyalty. The first sub-part under loyalty is "adjusting my schedule to meet the needs of those I am serving." The animal featured in this section is the great horned owl, which "demonstrates loyalty by building its schedule around the needs of its young." The scripture character is Amasa, a general who was disloyal to his uncle, King David. His disloyalty and consequent demise was brought about because he failed to adjust his schedule to meet the needs of those he was called to serve.

The other sub-parts under loyalty and the animals and Bible characters used to illustrate each are:

Standing with those I am serving in their time of need, illustrated by the Canadian goose and Mordecai;

Being a reliable messenger to those I am serving, illustrated by the honeybee and the Rechabites;

Knowing and following the wishes of those responsible for me, illustrated by the grizzly bear and Elisha.

The other major sections of the book are devoted to the themes of responsibility, courage, determination, orderliness, initiative, and decisiveness.

The book is described as a "new" approach to learning, restoring God's basic objectives. "The great challenge of our day," the book says, "is to grasp the concept of being mighty in spirit and to see how it differs from being directed by intellect. When one is mighty in spirit he has the ability to comprehend both the deeper thoughts of God and the hidden motives of man. The practical application of this is illustrated in the lives of such men as John the Baptist who was mighty in spirit and Stephen whose spirit of wisdom the entire assembly could not resist. The multitudes and the professions came to John to learn practical wisdom and counsel for their lives and their work. In our day we have unknowingly accepted a standard of education which hinders and destroys the potential of being mighty in spirit and emphasizes the idea that the highest achievement in education is to be guided by intellect."

The over-all purpose of the book is nothing less than to revolutionize the whole pattern of education for Christians so that God's objectives in learning are restored. To accomplish this Gothard lists three concepts:

1. *The home must be the learning center.*

"God's educational objectives were designed to be carried out in the home long before anyone ever thought about a school," says Gothard. "The school can be an effective extension of the home but can never take its place. Educators realize that the most effective learning is achieved in living experiences rather than classroom theory. The difficulty has come in that parents often do not have the alertness or the ability to turn everyday situations into teaching experiences."

The purpose of *Character Sketches* is to increase the parents' alertness and ability to make the home a learning center.

2. *The father must be responsible for teaching.*

"God never intended for a father to lose his role as a teacher," says Gothard. "As a father or grandfather scripture commands him to 'Teach ... thy sons and thy son's sons' (*Deuteronomy 4:9*). If a son or daughter ceases to look to their father as a 'teacher' they lose one of the most vital and lasting relationships in their lives. But in order for him to have this position his sons and daughters must want to learn from him. Thus it is his responsibility to win their confidence, think through what he intends to share, and create curiosity in their minds. He must expect to earn the privilege of teaching—not demand the right to do so. If a father has 'lost his audience' because of division or disharmony in the home, it is all the more important that he work to regain it."

3. *Mealtimes must include discussion of life concepts.*

"Behind almost every decision that your son or daughter faces are underlying concepts which are either scriptural or unscriptural," says Gothard. "It is essential that you not just give your opinion, but rather that you identify and analyze each concept upon which their decision is based."

Addressing the fathers, Gothard continues, "This means that you must first search out God's concepts in each area of life from scripture and from the counsel of wise men. Then you must be aware of the subtle undermining which constantly takes place against God's thinking. The wise father will expose the destructiveness of the world's thinking, before his sons and daughters become emotionally attached to a decision to follow them."

One of the most powerful tools against any concept is mocking, says Gothard. "Those in the world usually mock God's standards before presenting their alternative views," he says. "Either your children will have a godly contempt for the philosophies of the world or they will have an ungodly reaction to the ways of God which you have been seeking to teach. During the mealtime, the father must be skilled in showing a godly and wise contempt for the logical-sounding but distorted conclusions of the world with a clear reinforcing of scriptural concepts which the very spirit of their children reaffirm."

Gothard also gives directions as to how this book is to be used. Its purpose is not unlike that of Luther's catechism, which—contrary to the purpose for which it is often used today—was not written for children, but for parents to use *as they teach their children.* Gothard, more specifically—and in line with his concept of chain of authority— suggests that the book *"remain in the father's possession and under his supervision until all the concepts are discussed with all the family."*

Following are the specific suggestions given to fathers for the use of the book:

"We suggest that you select one meal each week during which you discuss the scriptural concept of one chapter. Begin the meal by informally asking the concept question for the chapter you are considering."

There are a total of 28 concept questions—one for each of the four sub-parts under each of the seven major parts of the book. A few examples of these concept questions are:

"If you were responsible for one thousand soldiers and your general told you to pursue the enemy who had equal strength, but you know that tomorrow you would have twice as many men, what would you do?

"If you were living under the rule of a mean and wicked leader and you overheard two of his assistants plotting to kill him what would you do?

"If your grandfather left instructions before he died that you were not to live in a certain city but a mission board wanted to send you there, what would you do?

"If a friend gave you a box of record albums to throw away which were causing him to stumble spiritually, and you found a few Christian-type songs among them which could be used in the music library at church, what would you do?"

After each of the questions there is a page number where the Bible story is found from which the correct answer is to be drawn.

Gothard's suggestions for the use of the book continue:

"Ask each person around the table what he would do in that situation. Don't force anyone to answer and don't allow anyone to ridicule another's answer. Allow the discussion to continue as long as the interest is maintained. Then after the meal, read the scripture story that corresponds to the concept question. See which one can identify the character in the story first. After reading the story encourage anyone to make further comment on it. Then explain the unique feature of the animal of that chapter which illustrates the character quality in the story. After this dismiss your family, but if some want to learn more about the nature story or the scripture story, you can give them the additional material in the chapter which is designed for this purpose."

There is no doubt about it, the concept of the book is most intriguing. The quality of printing, illustrations, layout and binding are impressive. The four pages in each of the 28 sections that deal with "animal story" are filled with fascinating biological information. For instance the four pages devoted to the woodcock include 10 illustrations, depicting interesting items about some distinctive and unusual physical characteristics of the bird. The text gives answers to 18 questions asked about the woodcock:

What do a woodock and a timber doodle have in common? What makes a woodcock's vision different from that of other birds? What is binocular vision? What could catch a woodcock? Which is larger, the male or female woodcock? What motivates a woodcock to work after dark? How long does it take before a woodcock can learn to fly? Is the woodcock a long-distance flyer? Where are a woodcock's ears? Can a woodcock see underground? How can a woodcock hear with its feet? How does a woodcock get the worm without the mud? How does it know when it has a worm in its bill? What would a woodcock do if an enemy approached? Would it be difficult to spot a woodcock? How does a woodcock whistle? How does a male use its wings to attract a mate? What is the woodcock's most deadly enemy?

It's easy to see that a book like this would be most entrancing to a young, inquisitive mind. All the more reason to wonder why Gothard has decided to make the book rather hard for the curious youngster to get to, since he suggests that the book "remain in the father's possession and under his supervision until all the concepts are discussed with all the family."

One can readily get excited about the live discussion that could take place around a family meal by following the concepts of this book. That's certainly to be preferred over a quick gulping down of the food to get back to the television set. And for those who would argue that it's unrealistic to hope for this kind of idea, there is the reminder that perhaps one reason the family likes to get away from the dinner table in a hurry is because the conversation is dull. Give them something worth staying for, and they will stay. Many prominent people who have led exciting lives testify that one of the important dimensions of their exciting lives was the family conversations they held around the dinner table. Gothard should be applauded for providing a tool such as the quality book *Character Sketches* for the enrichment it will bring to families around the dinner table.

Every purchaser gets an identification label to paste on the flyleaf of the book. On the label is a place to write his order name, and a number that has already been printed. Another part of that label, containing your name, address, and your intended use of the book plus the number is kept in the files of the Institute in Basic Youth Conflicts. For instance the number of my book is 4582. The Institute has a record of the fact that that book has been purchased by me.

Undoubtedly *Character Sketches* is the first in a series of books. Very likely the schedule with which other books will follow will depend somewhat on the sale of the first book, but if the eagerness I saw at Detroit is typical, then the future is not in doubt.

Gothard is firmly convinced that all subjects can be taught from a Christian perspective. For instance, history can be taught other ways than chronologically, he says. The chief thing about history is not to have the exact factual information of what happened in each century from the beginning of time. It is more important to know what happened to those people who followed God's plan and to those who didn't. Following the pattern of *Character Sketches* which tells something about the biological habits of certain animals and what that teaches us about such concepts as loyalty, responsibility, courage, determination, orderliness, initiative, and decisiveness, a similar approach might be used to teach history and to give positive and negative examples of peoples and nations who were either loyal or disloyal, responsible or irresponsible, courageous or cowardly, orderly or disorderly.

Gothard has not given a public announcement of future plans of his organization. I have the feeling from things I have heard him say at seminars that this is the direction in which he is heading. He has also indicated that many educators are enthralled with his theories and would welcome this kind of educational program. They are aware that they would have difficulty getting such a heavily religiously-oriented program of education adopted in public schools because of the separation of church and state, but it is quite possible that the increasing number of church-operated private schools may incorporate this principle in their teaching.

What do I think of it? I'm not an educator. Nor is Gothard the only educator. I'm sure there are other competent educators equally dedicated to Christ who would have some questions about the approach even though they also are disturbed by the fact that much of our education today does not produce quality character.

Chapter **12**

GOTHARD IN PERSPECTIVE

A Divine Sense of Humor

My first intention was to title this last chapter "The Pros and Cons of Bill Gothard," but "pros and cons" has a judgmental quality about it. It implies a decision that some things are good and some things are bad; some things are useful, others are not. But good or bad, useful or not useful for whom? And in relation to what? What may not be particularly useful for me may be very useful for someone else. That already is very obvious from the fact that some of Gothard's concepts with which I have difficulty seem to be extremely meaningful to many others. And some of Gothard's principles and approaches I find more useful than those recommended by others.

I've decided that it's not for me to tell others what they should or should not do in relation to Gothard. Realistically, I doubt that it would do very much good anyway.

To view something from a certain perspective, however, puts the onus on the reader. I will still make it quite clear where I stand, and how the situation looks from where

I stand. Others can judge the accuracy of my view if they will stand with me for a moment and determine if they see what I see. If they do, then at least my vision has been accurate. They may still not like what they see, in which case they can stand at a place better to their liking and view Gothard from there. The readers, therefore, will be forced into a double judgment, first of all to judge the accuracy of my observations, and then to determine if what I point out is more useful or less useful to them than another point of view might be.

No matter how much we may like to believe that our Christian convictions are based solely on our reading of the scriptures and how the Holy Spirit has led us on the basis of that reading, the fact is that when we read those scriptures we carry with us our individual backgrounds, which have been shaped by a complex intertwining family background, psychological conditioning, and—let's be honest—not a small amount of outright rationalization. The marvel of the power of the Spirit and the scriptures is that despite all these things God still gets through to us.

Again, the doctrine of Grace comes to our rescue. If we could be saved only by the certainty that we are 100% correct in all of our insights we could never be certain of our salvation. We all know friends, scholars, deeply committed Christians, many of whose views we share, but there are also some points with which we do not agree. If we had to agree that either they are wrong or we are wrong, and that therefore either they are not saved or we are not saved, we would indeed end up with a small band of Christians. It brings to mind the old Quaker humorism, "I think everybody is a bit queer except thee and me and sometimes I even have my doubts about thee."

This is not to say that it doesn't make any difference what you believe and that one "brand" of Christianity is just as good as any other. I heard a theologian say recently, "There is more than one way of explaining the Gospel, but that is not the same as saying that any old way will do." We are, therefore, called upon to exercise a sizable measure of humility when we judge our own Christian insights and compare them with those held by others.

I would also like to think that God has a sense of humor about all of this. If He can sit in the heavens and laugh while the heathen rage *(Psalm 2)*, I think He's capable of an occasional smile as Christians spar with each other, each insisting that his understanding is better than that of the other person.

The idea that God must have a sense of humor about all of this came to me in a rather overpowering way in 1956 when I had a three-month assignment in Germany on the staff of the Kirchentag, a lay movement of German Christians that became strong after World War II.

The Kirchentag was a huge biennial gathering of Christians for intensive Bible study, worship, and discussion of practical Christian living and its implication for all the areas of life. The leaders in the movement were those who had themselves undergone imprisonment for their faith and had spent time in concentration camps, where some of them had seen close friends and members of their family put to death. The strength of their faith had become a sign of hope for the world.

The Kirchentag had become something of an international and ecumenical event. Numerous Christians, particularly pastors and their wives from the United States, attended the Kirchentag and participated in the Bible studies and other events. For the most part the piety of the Americans held that smoking was sinful. Wives of German pastors smoked like chimneys. The German Christians had a different standard of piety. For them wearing cosmetics and having attractive hairdos was not altogether in character for one who wanted to be a first-rate Christian.

So here we had plain-faced, straight-haired, cigarette-smoking, nicotine-stained German Christian women looking somewhat askance at chicly-dressed, sharply-coiffeured, neatly-manicured American Christian women and having doubts about the depth of their faith, and the American women being equally concerned about the faith of their

German sisters. I simply insist that God must have a sense of humor about this.

In somewhat similar fashion it's only fair to report that Bill Gothard and I are just a bit nervous about each other. We both recognize each other as Christians, but as Bill said to me in our four-hour interview, "So many things that you say and believe are so close to the borderline that one could easily be led astray." Although in the previous chapters of this book I have already alluded to the things in Gothard's approach that many people find extremely helpful, and have affirmed my belief that Gothard deals with important areas of life often left unexamined by mainline churches who are much closer to my own way of thinking, I also feel that many of the things he says are also very close to the borderline of leading people to bondage rather than freedom.

Bondage Rather than Freedom

I double-checked with a number of professional counselors and they again told me that both they and their colleagues experience an increase in caseload whenever Gothard comes to town. As I mentioned in an earlier chapter, that in itself is not automatically bad. For instance, if an article appears in the paper that describes the symptoms of a particular kind of cancer—which can be cured if detected early enough—and the next week there is a huge upswing in doctor's appointments, that's good, not bad. When, however, it happens over and over again that an appearance of Gothard bulges the caseload of counselors, one at least needs to ask why.

For the most part the problems have to do with guilt, particularly in three areas. Gothard makes much of the fact— as does the Bible too—that if you have wronged someone, you should seek that person's forgiveness. In a day when offenses and forgiveness are taken altogether too cavalierly, this is not an unwholesome reminder. A too-heavy emphasis on this, however, can lead to further bondage and not the kind of freedom that forgiveness would bring.

A well-known researcher on youth problems described a conversation with a psychotherapist who also told of her increased caseload whenever Gothard came to town. In evaluating the situation the researcher said, "In general there are three responses to the Gothard program. 1. There are those who already have a rather rigid and legalistic view of life. When they go to Gothard, this rigidity is increased, and they are quite comfortable with having reinforced what they already believe. 2. A second group is a very open and healthy group. They go to Gothard and they are impressed with the good things. They take them, find them useful and benefit by them. The things they don't agree with they simply leave, without any feeling of guilt at not having accepted everything Gothard had to say. In the overall, they have a positive feeling. 3. A third group has more of a problem. This includes people of low ego strength. They already have a low opinion of themselves. And now they have another law laid on them and they can't meet these demands either, so they experience yet another failure. Instead of hearing a Gospel that freed them from guilt, they heard a law that laid more guilt on them."

One pastor told me that he had received a couple of midnight phone calls from a young person who had just attended a seminar and who was now impressed that he had to go to all the people he had ever wronged and confess his wrong to them. The youth was distraught and beside himself with the thought of all the people he had to go to, in many cases having forgotten both who the people were and what the offense was except just a vague recollection that he had done something wrong. "We had to do considerable counseling with this boy who was on the verge of a breakdown to give him a better understanding of forgiveness," the pastor said. This in itself may well have resulted in a wholesome experience, but it does raise the question of what could have happened to multitudes of others who may not have had the opportunity to get this counseling.

A second area of problems that fills the counselors' offices has to do with broken engagements. Since Gothard depends so very strongly on absolute parental approval of marriages, even though the young themselves are deeply devoted Christians and the parents who object may have nothing to do with Christianity, a number of deeply committed Christian engaged couples feel they have to break their engagements and so seek additional counseling. No one quarrels with the fact that it is far better to have parental approval than not to have it. But there are those who feel that even this principle must have some flexibility about it, flexibility that Gothard's completely closed system absolutely denies.

One of the puzzling aspects of Gothard's many success stories, in which he illustrates the happy ending that came about because the young couple did follow his plan of adjusting to parental wishes, is that these unchristian parents have amazing insights into what would make a good marriage and that the reason they are opposing a marriage is always because they have the best interests of their son or daughter at heart.

Little purpose is served by Gothard's telling success stories and my telling non-success stories to counter them. We will both be prejudiced and choose the kind of stories that will illustrate the point we wish to make. This very fact, however, of the *basic unfairness*—and harsh as the words may seem, I choose them carefully and deliberately— of being so selective in stories that the best of one situation is always compared with the worst of another situation, needs to be kept in mind if you are really interested in perspective.

Of course, Gothard and anyone else can find all kinds of stories that illustrate his point. The plain fact, however, is that there are also many instances in which a genuine attempt was made on the part of a young couple to be reasonable with unchristian parents and it did *not work out,* and there are instances where his suggestions were not followed and *it did work out.*

Other problems also come about because of Gothard's position of parental authority. The youth researcher referred to above told of a dedicated young Christian who wanted to be a youth worker. His father, however, thought that he should be a pastor. The young man was convinced that he did not have some of the characteristics a pastor ought to have and did have the abilities of a youth worker. He went to a Gothard Institute, and then, while a guest in the home of the youth researcher, said, "Well, I still would rather be a youth worker, but Gothard says I must always obey my parents, so I guess I'll become a pastor because that's what my father wants me to be."

"Look," the youth researcher told him, "you are 23 years old. When are you going to start taking some responsibility for your own life? You're not always going to have your father around to make your decisions for you." The young man decided to become a youth worker.

Gothard, of course, could speculate that if the young man followed his father's advice he might have found the pastoral office greatly to his liking and may have made an outstanding pastor. A number of similar stories probably could be found where this is precisely what happened. But again, what do you do with the large number of young people who have not developed a wholesome dynamic dialogue with parents, where there is equality of insight and not pulling of authoritarian rank?

Other Emphases Also Needed

He is under no compulsion to do the whole Christian task through his Institutes. Gothard is free to deliberately decide what his emphases will be.

1. *Perspective on social justice.* Because Gothard has focused so strongly on Proverbs and other wisdom literature, he has virtually no emphasis on the whole social justice with which the prophets are satiated. True, Gothard rightly points out that Paul and Jesus did adapt themselves to the social and economic structures of the day. Paul sent a slave back to his owner and urges slaves to be obedient to their mas-

ters. And Jesus nowhere started a Popular Liberation Organization to liberate Palestine from the Romans. In fact, it was precisely because he didn't do that that he was so misunderstood by the people of his day, including the disciples.

Nevertheless a reading of the prophets or Jesus' miracles gives overwhelming evidence that God is concerned with justice for the downtrodden. Otherwise, what shall we say of the great judgment scene in Matthew 25? Although other scriptures emphasize being saved by faith in Christ, the issue here that separated those who inherited eternal life and those who didn't, seems to be their works. Did they feed the poor, clothe the naked, minister to the sick and those in prison?

When I attended the seminar it was a little difficult for me to see how in a day when there are huge social upheavals on a world scale, with injustice crying from many quarters, a large gathering of Christians can meet for an entire week, talking about God's work in the world and not talk at all about social responsibility.

Farmers and doctors and lawyers and businessmen and women and the representatives of many other occupations who attend the Institute in Basic Youth Conflicts can be so imbued with the superiority of the spiritual over the material that they live in two different and conflicting worlds. Gothard insists on a balance, and the emphasis always is that imbalance occurs when too much emphasis is placed on the material and not enough on the spiritual. An equally damaging imbalance can result when not enough emphasis is given to the fact that the *earth* too is the Lord's and that our professional and occupational life *is as important as* our spiritual life.

2. *Perspective on ambiguity.* Perhaps the dentist was right when he said, "God didn't make any grays." But the fact is that many of them are not. This is particularly true in the business world. Here I am not referring to such obvious wrongs as cheating or lying. Right at this moment there is a

problems result when we look at gray and call it either black or white.

Much as we would like to believe that all decisions are between an obvious black and an obvious white, the fact is that many of them are not. This is particularly true in the business world. Here I am not referring to such obvious wrongs as cheating or lying. Right at this moment there is a long and intense argument in my home state on the right of a steel company to dump its waste either in the lake or at one of two land sites. The argument is that the waste product has a long-term danger if dumped in the lake or on one of the land sites. The argument of the company is that, first of all, the proof is not that well-documented that the waste is indeed dangerous to health. Furthermore the company says that a move to the other site would be so expensive that they would have to go out of business. If that should happen, many people who now earn a living at the factory will be out of a job.

People equally dedicated to the truth can be found in support of either side of the issue. Right and wrong are not so readily obvious even to the best of Christians. We are not saying that there aren't many instances where there is an obvious wrong and an obvious right, but often we must decide which is the lesser of two evils. We are dishonest if we insist that there is no such thing as ambiguity and that those who argue for it are simply trying to find an excuse for wrong doing.

We are human beings who are finite and sometimes sinful. But we also have to make decisions, and many decisions have to be made before all the facts are in. We would like to wait for more facts, but we simply don't have them. And yet we have to decide.

When those times come, we must make the decision to the best of our ability, and if we make a mistake, God in His grace forgives. It's better to honestly admit this than to continue to maintain that there is no such thing as ambiguity.

3. *Perspective on dialogues with the church.* Many churches are greatly impressed with what Gothard is doing, even though they may not agree wholly with his teaching. They can see that young people are being helped to a far greater degree through the seminars than through the local church programs. Churches would like to be as effective and could learn from Gothard.

On the other hand, I expect that some churches would like to have dialogue with Gothard in order to clear up areas of difference. In this way, both groups could present a solid front to the world and undoubtedly be more effective.

The Place of Reason

This whole matter of critical, but constructive, dialogue has troubled me throughout the book. Gothard, in the past at least, has discouraged people from openly discussing the seminar notes and lecture, thus airing their agreements or disagreements. He has said that if there is a disagreement, the person at the seminar should come to him, but there are great difficulties of doing this with such large audiences. And even when finally confronted with an objection, Gothard, according to one alumnus, doesn't show how his position is more reasonable, but merely falls back on his intepretation of scripture. Then he takes any further objection to be an attack on the Bible, not a questioning of his own interpretation. There seems to be more interest in the conclusions that Christians reach than in how those beliefs were established as true in the first place. Namely, there is more interest in the *authority* of the Bible than in whether it is *reasonable* to believe the Bible to be true.

Gothard has a very low opinion of reason. This comes out especially in his views on education where he says (in *Character Sketches*) that one should not "emphasize the idea that the highest achievement in education is to be guided by the intellect." He also suggests that fathers should encourage "a godly contempt for the philosophies of the world."

And he would probably substantiate these statements with I Corinthians 3:19—"For the wisdom of this world is foolishness with God."

Now indeed there is a lot of foolishness in this world that is passed off as wisdom, so I have no quarrel with that. My problem comes when Gothard thereby assumes that reason itself is suspect and ought to be displaced by scripture. I don't think the choice is between reason and scripture, but between reason and blind acceptance of authority.

Scripture is first in order of importance and therefore has the authority, but reason must be brought to bear on scripture in order for a person to discern whether it warrants our acceptance as authority.

Christians demand reasonable grounds for accepting secular information as authoritative, but are strangely afraid to allow this questioning attitude to carry over to spiritual matters. Perhaps they are afraid that scripture will fall short if it is examined. Or that they will lose their aggressive certainty if they entertain doubts. Or that they will be impious if they question the truth of God's Word.

I see no cause for worry, because scripture through the years has been able to withstand critical evaluation. God is the author of truth and it is not surprising to find that if we try to understand it, we will find it reasonable. As to losing one's aggressive certainty, what is wrong with a little tentativeness that says, "The Bible is God's revelation to me. It is not an outlined presentation of truth, but 66 books of stories, songs, proverbs, prophecies and letters that need to be read and reread to get the total picture. I am a finite person who is constantly adding to my understanding of scripture."

Often the problem with many Christians is that they have accepted scripture as true because someone else has told them so. And because they themselves haven't seriously grappled with whether the Bible is true, they are extremely uncomfortable about any confrontation. It is far easier to appeal to the Bible's authority, than to carefully demonstrate its reasonableness.

Dangers of Not Critically Evaluating Our Beliefs

1. We are taught from childhood that the Bible is the Word of God, but if we never ask why this is so, then our witness is confined to those who also believe the Bible is God's Word. We cannot use scripture to convince anyone who refuses to accept it as God's Word. Nor can we appeal to the Bible's authority when talking with a Moslem. He can prooftext right back from the Koran. On this level we can no longer appeal to authority; we must try to show why it is more *reasonable* to accept the Bible as our authority.

2. We cannot appeal to glowing examples of changed lives and seeming miracles to make our beliefs more plausible. Every religion and sect and cult has its amazing stories, and if we may want to question their sincerity or authenticity, we should remember that they have every right to question ours. Sooner or later theology by anecdote is seen for what it is, manipulation, no matter who it is who engages in it.

3. Critical evaluation is threatening, and it ought to be, for it may be that we will find our beliefs are not defensible. But if we fail to scrutinize our assumptions then we very easily fall victim to half truths, blind spots, unclear thinking, hidden presuppositions and personal biases. The sooner we root out erroneous beliefs, the sooner we can replace them with true ones.

4. When we begin to let others do our thinking for us, we lay ourselves open to believing anything because we won't even notice falsehoods and inconsistencies.

5. If we fail to allow criticism or dialogue then we will very often have to closely guard how we word particular statements about our beliefs. We will always be afraid that people will misunderstand our position unless we are

right there to defend and lead them at every turn. But when individual statements in a valid framework of belief are *themselves* true, they ought to sound reasonable enough to ring true to the listener as well. Furthermore our own beliefs, if true, will take on fuller meaning and life application as we openmindedly try to square them with other true beliefs we have. God is the author of truth and we may be confident that all true statements will be consistent with each other, for God is *not* the author of confusion.

A *Final Note*

Although Gothard and I have some serious disagreements, I hope that you the reader will be able to discern whether I have been as compassionate and objective as possible in this book. Gothard will keep referring us to Matthew 18 to show that public critical evaluation is not God's way, but may I point out that the text also says in verse 17 that if private dialogue and dialogue with witnesses fails to bring about the needed correction, then the Christian should take the matter to the church. Hopefully you, the reader, will accept this book on these grounds, and honor me in turn with your consideration of whether my statements square with the truth.

A key question is, how much latitude is there for Christians to disagree and still accept each other as Christian brothers and sisters? For me there is a fair amount of latitude. I have the feeling that Gothard would allow almost as much latitude. I consider him a Christian brother. Some of his program and emphases impress me very positively; others do not. He evidently is meeting the needs of many people. For this, God be praised.

My own personal view—and this is at least partially shaped by my heritage—is that I find greater excitement and inducement for victorious Christian living and service in the Kingdom of God in places and movements other than Bill Gothard's Institute in Basic Youth Conflicts. But for others, with different backgrounds and needs, they will find great strength, insight, and challenge in the Institute.

The one perspective out of which I view the whole Christian experience is the perspective of freedom that comes out of the Gospel: that God has accepted me as I am; that He has forgiven and continues to forgive my sins; and that we have a daily encounter in which I receive both His grace and His demands of discipleship.

In the scripture I also find guidelines on how I can live a responsible life. My salvation and my joy in life, however, come not from understanding His principles but in experiencing His love, using my intelligence to the best of my ability, dedicating myself to His service, and trusting in His forgiveness. My perspective of God's perspective is that while law and gospel are both important, the Gospel is central. And the Gospel leads to freedom, which is to be exercised responsibly.

OTHER BOOKS FROM QUILL PUBLICATIONS YOU'LL WANT TO READ

RAPID READING NATURALLY: WHAT IT IS, HOW TO TEACH IT

Ben E. Johnson

With this book and a desire to improve your reading speed, you can more than double your rate quickly and teach others to do the same.

ISBN 0-916608-00-X—$6.95 hardbound

MANAGEMENT FOR THE CHRISTIAN WORKER

Olan Hendrix

A positive and supporting book for the secular worker and manager who is a Christian, as well as the pastor or Christian administrator.

ISBN 0-916608-01-8—$6.95 hardbound

WHAT WAS THAT VERSE AGAIN?

Ben E. Johnson

Memory improvement methods for the Christian worker covering scripture memorization techniques for remembering all those things you wish you had remembered before.

ISBN 0-916608-08-5—$5.95 hardbound